The Very Easy Guide
To Knitting Scarves

The Very Easy Guide
To Knitting Scarves

Step-by-Step Techniques, Easy-to-Follow Patterns, and 22 Projects to Get You Started

Marie Connolly

St. Martin's Griffin
New York

A QUARTO BOOK

First edition for North America published in
2011 by St. Martin's Press.

All inquiries should be addressed to:
St. Martin's Press,
175 Fifth Avenue, New York, N.Y. 10010
www.stmartins.com

Library of Congress Cataloging-in-Publication
data available on request.

ISBN: 978-0-312-5-9077-2

First U.S. edition: October 2011

10 9 8 7 6 5 4 3 2 1

QUAR.SKCR

Conceived, designed, and produced by
Quarto Publishing plc
The Old Brewery
6 Blundell Street
London N7 9BH

Senior editor: Diana Craig
Art editor: Emma Clayton
Designer: Julie Francis
Design Assistants: Kate Bramley,
    Alison van Kerkhoff
Illustrator: Kuo Kang Chen
Technical editors: Betty Barnden,
    Betty Willetts
Indexer: Helen Snaith
Art director: Caroline Guest
Creative director: Moira Clinch
Publisher: Paul Carslake

Color separation in Singapore by Pica
Digital Pte Ltd
Printed in Singapore by Star Standard
International Pte Ltd

Contents

Introduction

What was your first knitting project? Most likely it was a scarf, for these knitted pieces are where many of us start and often return. Scarves never lose their appeal. Simply cast on with your favorite yarn and needles and you're on the way to creating something beautiful.

My goal for this book was to create patterns that elevate and transform the simple rectangular scarf. With each new design, I challenged myself to push the limit to create 22 new scarves—scarves with a big difference! I wanted to show how, by changing the shape, yarn, and stitch used for this most humble of knitted garments, the variations are unexpected and infinite. For example, in the Climbing Vines shawl, I show how to transform a simple lace scarf by pairing a traditional lace pattern with an unconventional choice of a chunky yarn. In Crown Jewels and Knitted Bib, I change our perceived notions of what a scarf can be.

As you page through the scarves, you will find that while they are steeped in traditional knitting stitches like cables and lace, the patterns are up to the minute syle-wise. The time-honored Fair Isle patterns in the Prince Charming design are reinterpreted by making it a infinite loop. Or the chunky cable-knit, Cables and Baubles, is made ultra-feminine by adding eyelets and ribbons. Each yarn choice illuminates the stitch work.

Projects range from easy to advanced. For the beginner knitter, I explore basic stitches paired with beautiful yarns to create gorgeous scarves. For the more advanced knitter, I venture into lace patterning, Fair Isle knitting and embroidered embellishments that will inspire even the most jaded scarf knitter to pick up his or her needles. In these pages, you'll find brilliantly photographed patterns paired with expertly illustrated instructions. If you still want more, I also go beyond the basics of just knitting from a pattern to designing your own scarf.

So pick up your needles and let's get wrapped up in scarves.

Marie Connolly

About this book

Step-by-step techniques ▶

In each chapter, a section of step-by-step instructions explains the basic knitting techniques needed to make the scarves that follow.

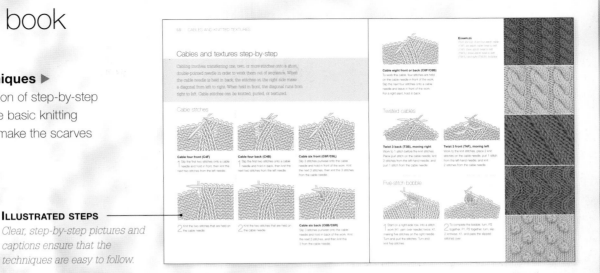

ILLUSTRATED STEPS

Clear, step-by-step pictures and captions ensure that the techniques are easy to follow.

◀ Libraries

Each chapter has its own library of stitch patterns. These may be used to customize the different scarves, allowing you to create infinite variations on the patterns in the book. For understanding abbreviations and reading symbols, turn to page 26.

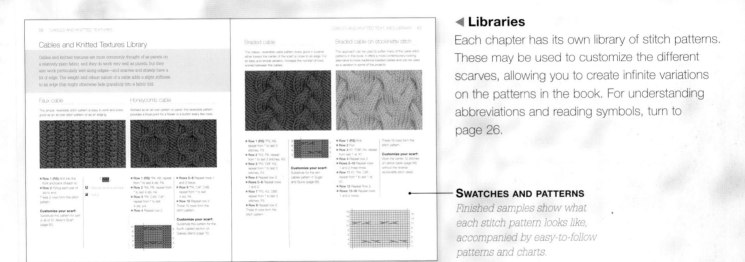

SWATCHES AND PATTERNS

Finished samples show what each stitch pattern looks like, accompanied by easy-to-follow patterns and charts.

Patterns ▶

The 22 patterns in the book are divided into four different categories of stitch and technique: basic knit and purl, cables and knitted textures, colorwork, and lace. Inventive design and creative use of the different stiches and yarns ensure that each scarf has its own unique character.

CLEAR INFORMATION

Well laid-out instructions and complete lists of the tools and materials needed make the patterns easy to follow.

CHAPTER 1

The Basics

Before you can get creative with your knitting, there are a number of basics to consider. This chapter looks at such fundamentals as the choice of yarns and tools, demonstrates basic knitting techniques, and explains how to decode patterns, read charts, and ensure that you have the right gauge.

Choosing yarns

Sometimes picking yarn can be overwhelming. What color shall I choose? What yarn weight is correct? How much will I need? All these questions and more swirl around in your head. Here are my suggestions on selecting yarns for the scarves in this book. I hope my hints will empower you in your knitting.

Estimating quantities

First, it goes without saying that if you have a pattern and it gives an amount, buy that amount plus one skein. That might sound basic but even I sometimes start a project hoping that I'll eke out enough yarn. But what happens if you don't have a pattern but come across a yarn that you really love? Here are my basic guidelines for shopping at wool festivals and local yarn shops:

■ Fine and sportweight yarns: at least 400 yards (360 meters) but if I can swing it I get 800 yards (730 meters) that will insure I can make a fairly detailed shawl

■ DK and worsted-weight yarns: 400 (366) to 600 yards (550 meters)

■ Chunky- to bulky-weight yarns: 200 yards (180 meters)

Color and weight

Faced with the huge array of yarns on offer, which should you choose? My own personal process begins by determining the stitch pattern. Then I select the color that would best display the stitches. So, for example, cables will look better on brighter colors. I also love lace in a beautiful solid color because it shows off the stitches so well—see the Triangle Lace Shawl pictured on page 118.

Next I decide which weight of yarn to select. I'm willing to be unorthodox in these decisions. I believe a chunky yarn as used in the Climbing Vines Shawl on page 122 can demonstrate the beauty of lace stitching just as easily as a fine or sportweight yarn. Or I love cables over

Bamboo yarn

Wool and cotton yarn

Lambswool and alpaca yarn

Mohair and silk yarn

Cotton yarn

Merino wool yarn

Handspun tweed yarn

a range of yarn weights. They look great knit on both thin and bulky yarns; it all depends on the size and scope of the specific cable pattern. For example, I used a chunky yarn for Cables and Baubles (page 64) because the cables are oversized, but on Sugar and Spice (page 68), I chose a soft color and a medium-weight yarn to bring out the subtle beauty of each stitch.

Fiber

Although manmade fibers can produce some fun effects, I admit I work with natural fibers whenever possible. I love them all—alpaca, merino, cashmere, cotton, mohair, and silk. Then I start to knit a swatch. I practice the stitch pattern and check my gauge—the number of stitches per inch and how the fabric drapes. Some patterns, like the St. Alban's Scarf (page 50), require a crisp stitch definition, while others, like the Lace Ruffle Shawl (page 110), benefit from a softer drape.

Luxury yarns

Every once in a while, I splurge. I can't resist taking home a beautiful luxury yarn like beaded mohair or an artistically hand-painted yarn. I believe these splurge yarns can be inspirational. When I saw the beaded mohair, I knew immediately that I had to make something incredible to show off its beauty; thus the Knitted Bib (page 80) necklace was created.

My last words of wisdom for picking yarns is to enjoy your knitting. Knit what you like with yarns you love and your creations will be incredible!

Ball bands

Most yarns have a paper band or tag attached with vital information such as the weight of the ball or skein, fiber composition, yardage, and how to look after your finished item. The band may also recommend hook and needle sizes and give gauge details.

Manufacturer

Ball weight

Yardage

Gauge

Aftercare instructions

Yarn name

Fiber composition

Needle/hook sizes

Fur-effect yarn

Eyelash yarn

Self-striping sock yarn

Yarn from recycled fabric

Ribbon yarn

Bouclé yarn

Choosing your tools

You do not need complicated or expensive equipment to learn to knit—just knitting needles and yarn. As you progress in the craft, you can collect more equipment as you need it. Before you begin any knitting project read the materials section carefully to see what size knitting needles are required and what other equipment, if any, is needed.

Knitting needles

Knitting needles are an investment because you will use them time and time again. Look after your needles carefully and they will last for years, but when the points are damaged or the needles are bent, it is time to throw them out and buy new ones. To experiment with different yarns and gauges, you will need knitting needles in different sizes. You will also need a cable needle for working cable stitch patterns, and double-pointed needles or a circular needle if you want to try knitting in the round (see pages 14–15). A crochet hook is also useful for techniques such as provisional cast-on.

STRAIGHT KNITTING NEEDLES
Pairs of needles are made in a variety of lengths, ranging from around 10 in (25 cm) to 16 in (40 cm). Most knitting needles are aluminum, usually with a pearl-gray finish, though some are nickel-plated. Larger needles are made of plastic to reduce their weight. Bamboo needles are a flexible alternative.

CROCHET HOOK
A crochet hook can be used to rescue dropped stitches as well as to bind off.

CABLE NEEDLES
These are used for knitting cable stitch patterns. Some have a kink or crank to help keep the stitches on the needle.

Other useful items

The scarves in this book need different tools depending on the pattern being worked. However, you will need to have on hand a tape measure or ruler and scissors. A tapestry or knitter's needle, stitch holder, and row counter may be needed too, along with a few other notions that you may find indispensable.

NEEDLE GAUGE
This allows you to measure the size of your needles and may have metric sizes on one side and imperial on the other, as in this example.

ROW COUNTER
This handy little tool helps keep your place.

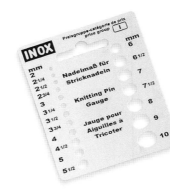

SCISSORS
Choose scissors that are not too small and not too large, but very sharp.

TAPE MEASURE
The most useful tape measures show both inches and centimeters on the same side, but stick to one measuring system as the equivalents are not exact.

NEEDLES FOR SEWING
You will need blunt-pointed needles—either tapestry or knitter's needles—in different sizes for different weights of yarn.

SPLIT MARKERS
Made from plastic, these split-ring markers are used to mark a particular stitch. They can be added and removed at any time.

POINT PROTECTORS
Little point protectors stop the stitches from falling off the needles if you have to leave your knitting in the middle of a row.

STITCH HOLDER
These long pins are used for holding groups of stitches until they are required.

BOBBINS
Bobbins are used to prevent multiple lengths of yarn from tangling together during intarsia color knitting.

POM-POM RINGS
Though not strictly necessary, pom-pom rings in different sizes make short work of creating decorative extras.

KNITTER'S THIMBLE
Worn on the index finger of the hand that holds the yarn, this is used for managing multiple lengths of yarn in stranded color knitting.

Circular needles

Consisting of two short conventional knitting needles joined by a thin flexible cord, circular needles can be used to knit in the round—enabling items such as bags or sweaters to be worked in a tubular fashion without seams—or to work backward and forward in rows, particularly useful when working on a large number of stitches.

How they work

Circular needles can be used to knit in rows in the same way as conventional knitting needles, and they are becoming increasingly popular, especially for working big projects such as throws or wraps. Circular needles are simply two short needle ends joined by a flexible nylon or plastic cord. The long linking cord enables large numbers of working stitches to be stored safely without the risk of dropped stitches. In addition, the weight of the work is distributed evenly along the cord, making heavy pieces easier to handle.

They are available in the same diverse range of materials as ordinary knitting needles. Stainless steel, aluminum, nickel-plated brass, and resin are all popular options, while bamboo needles are lightweight and warmer to the touch. The pliable cables are generally thin hollow plastic tubes that meet the needles in a smooth joint over which yarns can slide easily without snagging.

WORKING IN THE ROUND
Cast on the number of stitches required. Mark the beginning of the round by placing a ring marker or a loop of thread in a contrasting color onto the tip of the right-hand needle. Bring the needle ends together making sure the stitches are not twisted around the needle. Work the stitches from the left-hand needle onto the right-hand needle, pushing the stitches to be worked along the left-hand needle and the worked stitches down the right-hand needle, so all the stitches slip around the cord. When you reach the marker you will have completed one round. Slip the marker from the left-hand needle onto the right-hand needle and work the next round. The right side of the knitting is always facing you.

Double-pointed needles

These offer an alternative to circular needles. Double-pointed needles are sold in sets of four or five, and in several lengths. They were traditionally made of steel, but aluminum is more usual now, with bamboo and plastic in some sizes.

Double-pointed needles

Lace needles with extra-sharp tips

Lightweight bamboo needles

Polished metal needles with extra-light grips

Aluminum needles

Stainless steel needles

Choosing the right size

Circular needles come in a range of sizes that correspond with standard knitting needles, and in various cord lengths. The length of a circular needle is measured from needle tip to needle tip. Most sizes are in lengths of 16 in (40 cm) to 47 in (120 cm). The choice depends on the yarn and the number of stitches—the pattern you work from will state the size required. Special circular needles for lace knitting are generally made of lightweight, smooth metal with extra-long tapered tips and a completely smooth transition from needle to cord to protect fine yarns. Most circular needles are permanently fixed to the cord. However, there are circular needle systems now on the market, including some for lace knitting. These provide a range of different-sized needle tips together with alternative lengths of pliable cord that are easily interchangeable.

Tip

A circular knitting needle will accommodate stitches equivalent to approximately twice its length. Unless working the magic loop technique, the needle length should be about 4 in (10 cm) shorter than the circumference of the piece to be knitted. If too long a needle is used, the stitches will not easily slip around it, making knitting the stitches difficult and causing the knitting to stretch.

Holding yarn and needles

Knitting is a two-handed craft in which stitches are worked off the left needle and onto the right. There are many ways to hold and control the yarn and needles. Experiment with those suggested here until you find one that suits you. To get started, sit comfortably and relax. Knitting requires hand and eye coordination, which is hard to achieve if you are tense.

Holding the yarn

The yarn runs through and around the fingers, leaving the fingertips free to manipulate the needles and control the yarn. The holds shown right have been devised in order to feed the yarn onto the needle evenly. In each of the holds, the yarn feeds from the ball around the little finger, across to the index finger, from where the working yarn is wrapped around the right needle as required.

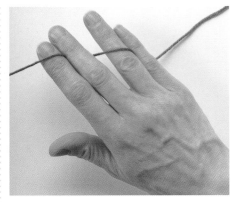

LOOSELY IN RIGHT HAND
To tension the yarn loosely, simply slip the yarn alternately over and under the fingers.

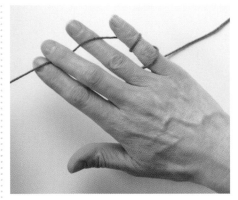

MORE FIRMLY IN RIGHT HAND
To tension the yarn more firmly, wrap the yarn around the little finger, then over and under the other fingers.

Tip

Controlling the yarn with the right hand is the method used in what is known as English knitting, and suits right-handed knitters; the yarn is guided by the right index finger. Left-handed knitters may find it easier to follow the Continental method, in which the yarn is held in the left hand.

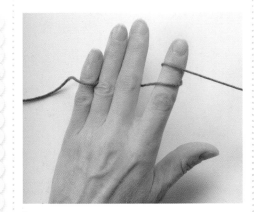

LOOSELY IN LEFT HAND
To tension the yarn loosely, try taking it over the little finger, under the next two, and around the index finger.

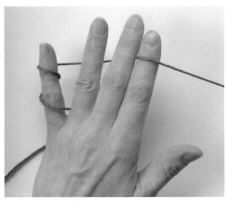

MORE FIRMLY IN LEFT HAND
To tension the yarn more firmly, wrap the yarn around the little finger, then under and over the other fingers

Holding the needles

Once you are holding the yarn, pick up a pair of needles, one in each hand, and try out these different holds. Some knitters hold the right needle like a pen; others hold it overhand like a knife. The left needle is usually held overhand. With the free-needle (or pen) hold, the needles used are as short as is practical, and the weight of the knitting on the right needle is supported by the hand and wrist. With the fixed-needle (or knife) hold, long needles are used, and the right needle is tucked under the arm for support.

FREE NEEDLE WITH YARN IN RIGHT HAND
With your right hand, pick up a needle and hold it like a pen. Take the other needle in your left hand, holding it lightly over the top. Try moving the needles forward and back with your fingertips, keeping your elbows relaxed at your sides. When you cast on and start knitting, do not drop the right needle to manipulate the yarn; instead, support it in the crook of your thumb and use your index finger to control the yarn.

FIXED NEEDLE WITH YARN IN RIGHT HAND
With your right hand, pick up a needle, hold it overhand like a knife, and tuck the end of the needle under your arm. Take the other needle in your left hand, holding it lightly over the top. Practice moving the left needle against the right. When knitting, you will find that you can let go of the right needle each time you make a stitch.

YARN IN LEFT HAND
Hold the needle in your right hand like a pen or knife as preferred; hold the needle in your left hand lightly over the top. When knitting, hold the yarn taut with the left hand and guide it with your left index finger, while hooking or catching it with the point of the right needle.

Getting started: Casting on

Before you begin your cast on, you first need to make a slip knot loop. This is placed on one needle and is counted as the first stitch. There are several methods of casting on. Those shown here are the most frequently used methods. Unless a pattern states a particular cast on, choose the one you are most comfortable with.

Making a slip knot loop

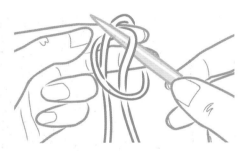

1 Leaving a long end, wind the yarn from the ball around two fingers of your left hand to form a circle. Pull a loop of yarn though it with one of your needles.

2 Pull the end from the ball of yarn to tighten the loop on the knitting needle. This loop forms your first stitch.

Casting on

Two-needle or cable cast-on

1 Hold the needle with the slip knot loop in your left hand and insert the right-hand needle into the loop from front to back. Take the loose yarn under the right-hand needle and up over the right needle.

2 Slide the right-hand needle back and toward you, drawing the yarn through the slip knot loop to make a new stitch, then transfer the loop to the left-hand needle.

3 Insert the right needle between the two stitches on the left needle. Take the yarn under the right needle and up between the needles. Draw a loop through and transfer the new stitch to the left needle. Continue to cast on by inserting the right needle between the last two stitches.

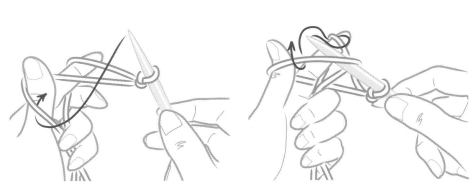

Long tail (Continental) thumb cast-on

1 Hold the needle with the slip knot loop in your right hand. Take the yarn from the ball over your left index finger and grip both ends of the yarn in your left palm. Insert the needle under the yarn across the front of your thumb.

2 Pass the needle over the yarn across your index finger, and draw the loop through the loop on your thumb. Remove your thumb and pull the ends of the yarn to tighten the stitch.

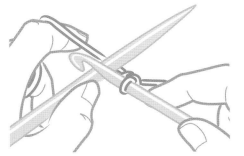

Provisional cast-on

1 Using a contrasting yarn, make a slip knot. Insert a crochet hook through the loop. With the hook in your right hand and the needle in your left hand, take the yarn behind the needle.

2 Wrap the yarn over the hook and draw through the loop on the hook. Take the yarn back behind the needle and repeat the sequence.

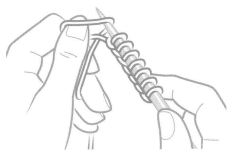

Backward loop (easy loop) cast-on

Make a slip knot on the needle. With the yarn in your left hand, make a loop around your thumb from front to back. Insert the needle into the loop from the front, slip your thumb out, and gently pull the yarn to make a stitch on the needle.

EXAMPLES
From the top: cable cast-on; contrast cable cast-on; contrast cable cast-on starting with a WS row; contrast thumb cast-on; thumb cast-on

Getting started: Knit and purl

Knit and purl stitch are the two basic knitting stitches and are used in various combinations to make up most stitch patterns. The fabric is worked in rows from right to left, transferring the stitches from the left-hand needle to the right-hand needle. At the end of each row the work is turned, ready to work the next row.

Knit stitch

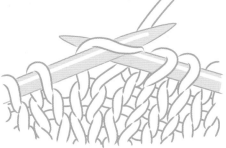 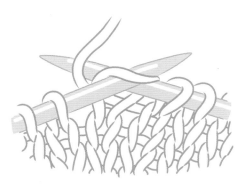 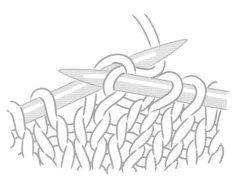

1 Hold the needle with the stitches in your left hand and the yarn from the ball in your right hand. Insert the right-hand needle into the first stitch on the left-hand needle from front to back.

2 Take the yarn under the right-hand needle, between the two needles, and over the right-hand needle.

3 With the right-hand needle draw the yarn through the stitch to form a new stitch on the right needle. Slip the original stitch off the left needle. Repeat until all stitches are on the right-hand needle.

Purl stitch

 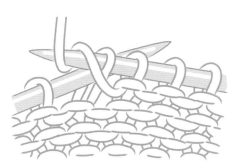 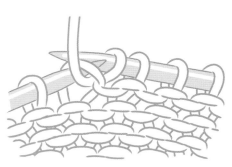

1 Hold the needle with the stitches in your left hand and the yarn from the ball in your right hand. Insert the right-hand needle into the first stitch on the left-hand needle from back to front.

2 Take the yarn over the right-hand needle, between the two needles, and under the right-hand needle.

3 With the right-hand needle draw the yarn through the stitch to form a new stitch on the right needle. Slip the original stitch off the left needle. Repeat until all stitches are on the right-hand needle.

Garter stitch

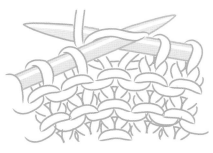

Working every row in either knit or purl stitches produces a simple, reversible fabric known as garter stitch.

Stockinette stitch

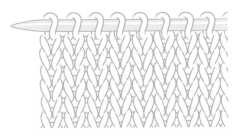

By knitting every right-side row and purling every wrong-side row a stockinette stitch fabric is produced.

Reverse stockinette stitch

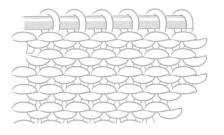

By purling every right-side row and knitting every wrong-side row a reverse stockinette stitch is produced.

Twisted knit and purl

To give a stitch a twisted appearance and make it firmer, work into the back of the loop.

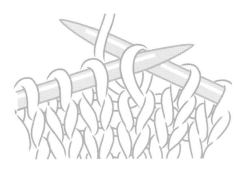

Knit through back of loop (ktbl)
Insert the right-hand needle into the back of the next stitch on the left-hand needle from front to back and knit it as usual.

Purl through back of loop (ptbl)
Insert the right-hand needle into the back of the next stitch on the left-hand needle from back to front and purl it as usual.

EXAMPLES

From the top: garter stitch; stockinette stitch; reverse stockinette stitch; twisted knit and purl; ridge stitch (alternating bands of stockinette and reverse stockinette)

Getting started: Shaping and binding off

By increasing or decreasing the number of stitches in a row, you can shape your work or create new stitch patterns, and binding off is essential to secure the last row of stitches so they don't unravel. Picking up stitches from an edge allows you to add a band or border in another direction, while Kitchener stitch offers a neat way of joining separate knitted pieces.

Increasing

Knit front and back (Kfb)
Knit into the front of the stitch but leave the stitch on the left needle and then knit into the back of the same stitch. Slip the stitch off the left-hand needle, making two stitches on the right-hand needle.

Yarn-over on a knit row (yo)
Take the yarn from back to front between the needles, then from front to back over the right needle and knit the next stitch. The yarn lays across the right-hand needle, making a loop which is worked as a stitch.

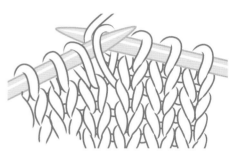

Make 1 (M1)
With the left needle, pick up the strand between the stitches on the needles from the front. The right leg of the strand should be at the front of the left needle. Knit into the back of it to make one new stitch.

Decreasing

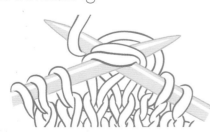

Knit 2 together (K2tog)
On a knit row, insert the right-hand needle into the next two stitches on the left-hand needle and knit the stitches together.

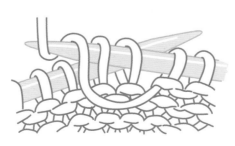

Purl 2 together (P2tog)
On a purl row, insert the right-hand needle into the next two stitches on the left-hand needle and purl the two stitches together.

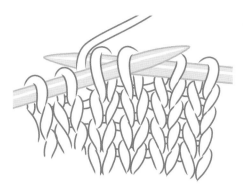

Slip, slip, knit (ssk)

1 Slip the next stitch on the left needle as if to knit, twice. Insert the left needle tip through the front loops of both slipped stitches together. Wrap the yarn around the right needle tip, as if to knit.

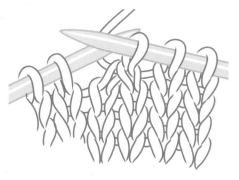

2 Knit the two slipped stitches together, leaving one new stitch on the right-hand needle.

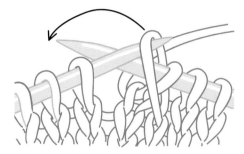

Slip 1, knit 1, pass slipped stitch over (skpo)

On a knit row, slip the next stitch as if to knit, then knit the next stitch. Use the point of the left-hand needle to lift the slipped stitch and pass it over the knit stitch and off the needle. The decrease slopes to the left on the right side.

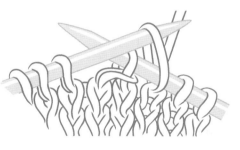

Slip 1, knit 2 together, pass slipped stitch over (sl1, K2tog, psso)

Slip the next stitch as if to knit, then knit the next two stitches together to decrease a stitch. Use the point of the left-hand needle to lift the slipped stitch and pass it over the knit stitch and off the needle to work the second decrease, which slopes to the left on the right side.

EXAMPLES

From the top: Kfb preceded by K2tog; M1 preceded by K2tog; K2tog followed by a yarn-over; K2togbtl preceded by a yarn-over; sl1, K2tog, psso with yarn-overs on either side.

Binding off

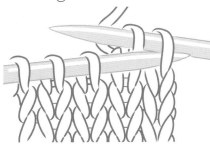
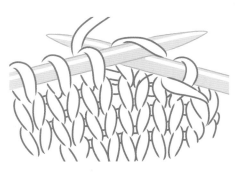
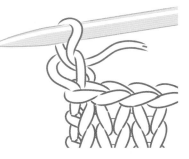

1 Work the first two stitches so that they are transferred onto the right-hand needle. Insert the left-hand needle, from left to right, into the front of the first stitch on the right-hand needle.

2 With the left needle, lift the first stitch over the second and off the needle. The first stitch has been bound off; the second stitch stays on the right needle. Knit the next stitch, lift and pass as above.

3 Continue to bind off in this way until one stitch remains on the right-hand needle. To secure, cut off the yarn about 4 in (10 cm) from the knitting, draw the end through the stitch, and pull to tighten.

Kitchener stitch (grafting stockinette stitch panels)

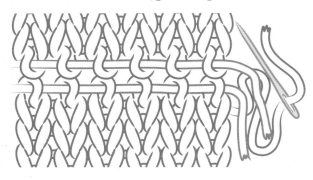
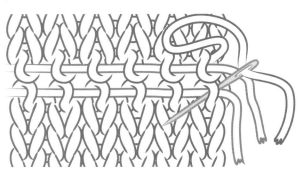

1 Lay the two edges flat, with right sides uppermost, with one long yarn tail at lower right, threaded into a tapestry needle. (It doesn't matter where the other yarn tail is.)

2 Bring the needle up from the back through the center of the first stitch on the upper edge (knitwise). Now bring the needle from the back, through the first stitch on the lower edge (purlwise).

3 Pull the yarn through gently. Pass the needle down through the center of the same upper stitch (purlwise), and up through the center of the next stitch (knitwise) in one movement.

4 Pull the yarn through. Pass the needle down through the center of the same lower stitch (knitwise) and up through the center of the next stitch (purlwise). Repeat steps 3 and 4, passing the yarn twice through each stitch loop. Always start with the last stitch worked, then pass the yarn through the next stitch along.

Picking up stitches

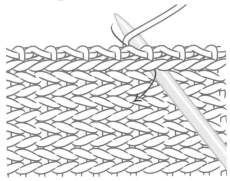

From a selvage edge

1 With the right side of the work facing, insert the needle tip one whole stitch in from the edge. If the side edge is made with a selvage stitch, as here, it's easier to see where to insert the needle.

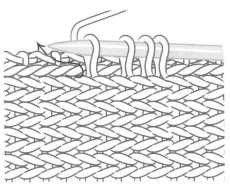

2 Wrap the yarn around the tip and draw the new loop through, making a new stitch on the needle. Repeat as required.

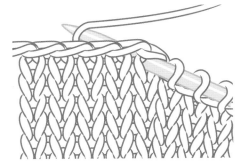

From a bound-off edge

With the right side of the work facing, insert the needle tip through the center of each stitch of the last row, wrap the yarn, and pull the new stitch through. Picking up one stitch in each stitch of a bound-off edge makes a neat, firm line.

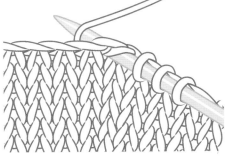

From a cast-on edge

With the right side of the work facing, insert the needle tip in the space between two stitches of the first row, wrap the yarn, and pull through.

EXAMPLES

From the top: contrast chain bind-off; contrast bind-off; picot bind-off; Kitchener stitch

Reading patterns

What do pattern abbreviations and repeat instructions mean? Reading a knitting pattern may be unfamiliar at first, but as soon as you have cracked the code, you will be able to follow instructions with confidence.

Before you start

Read through the whole pattern before you start knitting and check that you have everything you need. The pattern lists the yarn and other tools. It is important to buy the yarn specified. Another yarn, however similar, may not behave in the same way and you might need a different amount. If you have no choice but to substitute another quality of yarn, check that the yardage, or meterage, amounts to the same. And make sure that you buy enough—it is wise to buy a little more yarn than the pattern stipulates.

The pattern will also suggest needles to achieve the recommended gauge (see page 29), and indicate whether any additional equipment, such as cable needles or stitch holders, is required.

Abbreviations

Once you are familiar with abbreviations, you will find it quicker and easier to follow the instructions. Some abbreviations are simply the first letter of the word, such as "K" for "knit." Others use the first few letters, such as "rep" for "repeat." Sometimes the first letters of several words are run together—"skpo" for "slip one, knit one, pass the slipped stitch over." Not all knitting instructions use the same abbreviations. It is therefore important to read the abbreviations each time you follow a new set of instructions.

Repeats

Knitting is full of repetition. Stitch patterns repeat horizontally across a row and vertically over several rows. These multiples can either be shown on a chart or explained in words. Round or square brackets can be used to enclose instructions that are to be repeated. For example, "[K2, P2] 3 times" is a concise way to write "K2, P2, K2, P2, K2, P2."

Asterisks are also used as markers to indicate a repeat. For example, "rep from * to *" means "repeat the instructions contained between the asterisks the number of times specified." When two parts of a garment share the same instructions, a group of asterisks is used to indicate the sections that are the same and where they differ.

Abbreviations & symbols

The following abbreviations are common to knitting patterns. Special abbreviations appear elsewhere in the book, with the patterns to which they relate.

BC (Back cross) Slip 1 stitch onto cable needle and hold in back, K1, P1 from cable needle

C4B (Cable 4 back) Slip next 2 stitches from left-hand needle onto cable needle and hold in back; K next 2 stitches from left-hand needle; K2 from cable needle

C4F (Cable 4 front) Slip next 2 stitches from left-hand needle onto cable needle and hold in front; K next 2 stitches from left-hand needle; K2 from cable needle

C6F (Cable 6 front) Slip 3 stitches from the left-hand needle onto cable needle and hold in front; knit 3 from left-hand needle, 3 from cable needle

C6B (Cable 6 back) Slip 3 stitches from left-hand needle onto cable needle and hold in back, knit 3 from left-hand needle, 3 from cable needle

C8B (Cable 8 back) Slip 4 stitches on left-handed needle onto cable needle and hold in back; knit 4 from left-hand needle, 4 from cable needle

C8F (Cable 8 front rib) Slip 4 stitches on left-hand needle onto cable needle and hold in front; knit 1, purl 1 twice from left-hand needle; knit 1 purl 1 twice from cable needle

FC (Front cross) Slip 1 onto cable needle and hold in front, P1, K1 from cable needle

Inc Increase/increases/increasing

K Knit
Knit on RS, purl on WS

Kfb Knit into front and then back of stitch

K2tog Knit 2 stitches together

K2togw3 When knitting the next 2 stitches together wrap the yarn 3 times around the right-hand needle then complete the stitch

Kw3 When knitting the next stitch wrap the yarn 3 times around the right-hand needle, then complete the stitch

M1 Make 1 stitch: lift thread lying before next stitch and K it through back loop

MB Make bobble as given in instructions

P Purl
Purl on RS, knit on WS

P2tog Purl 2 stitches together

P2togtbl Purl 2 stitches together through the back of the loop

P3tog Purl 3 stitches together

Pfb Put into front and then back of stitch

Pm Place marker

Pso Pass stitch over

Psso Pass slipped stitch over next stitch on right-hand needle

Rem Remaining

Rep Repeat

RS Right side

RT (Right twist) Skip next stitch and insert needle into second stitch knitwise, draw up a stitch, then insert needle into skipped stitch and knit it, let both stitches fall from needle

Skpo Slip 1 knitwise, knit 1, pass slipped stitch over

Sk2togpo Slip 1 stitch, knit 2 stitches together, pass the slip stitch over

Slip 1 Slip next stitch purlwise or knitwise as stated in pattern

Sm Slip marker

Sp2po Slip 1 stitch, purl 2 together through the back of the loop, pass the stitch over

Ssk Slip next 2 stitches knitwise, yarn round needle, pass both slipped stitches over

St/sts Stitch/stitches

T4B (Twist 4 back or right) Slip next 2 stitches from left-hand needle onto cable needle and hold in back; knit next 2 from left-hand needle; purl 2 from cable needle

T4F (Twist 4 front or left) Slip next 2 stitches from left-hand needle onto cable needle and hold in front; purl next 2 stitches from left-hand needle; knit 2 from cable needle

Tbl Through the back of loops

W&T Wrap and turn: work to stitch as indicated, bring yarn to the front, slip 1 purlwise, bring yarn to back, slip stitch back to left-hand needle, turn work to other side

WS Wrong side

Wyib With yarn in back (as work faces you)

Wyif With yarn in front (as work faces you)

Yo Yarn over needle counterclockwise to make extra stitch

[....] Work what is between the brackets as directed

[* *] Repeat instructions between asterisks as directed

Reading charts

Charts are a visual explanation of stitches and rows. They are a very efficient way to check your place in a pattern repeat or to compare one repeat with another. Each square usually represents one stitch.

Numbered rows

Charts are always numbered from the bottom to the top, because this is the direction of the knitting. The first row may be either a right- or a wrong-side row. Right-side rows are read from right to left; wrong-side rows are read from left to right. The multiple of the pattern repeat is sometimes shown underneath the chart, while shaded areas or dotted lines indicate extra or end stitches.

Enlarging a chart by photocopying can make it easier to follow. Make several copies and glue or tape them together. If it helps, draw any shapings on the photocopy.

Charts with symbols

Every stitch and every row is shown as on the right side of the knitting. A blank square represents knit on a right-side row and purl on a wrong-side row—making stockinette. A dot represents purl on a right-side row and knit on a wrong-side row—making reverse stockinette. Some symbols represent more than one stitch, such as a decrease. Where the stitch count varies within a stitch pattern, solid areas compensate for the missing stitches. Not all methods of charting use the same symbols, so always check the key to the charts before you begin.

Color knitting charts

Most color knitting is in stockinette, so every right-side row is knit and every wrong-side row is purl, with the squares on the chart showing the color to be used. The chart may be printed in color or may use a symbol for each color. If any textured stitches are used, they will be shown as symbols and explained in the key.

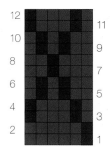

COLOR CHARTS
When working from a color chart, look not only at the sequence of stitches to come but also the color of the stitches in the row below. This makes it easier to place the colors accurately as well as to spot errors.

CHART REPEATS
Some stitch patterns have a bold line extending beyond the grid. The stitches to the right of this line are the repeat; the stitches to the left are any stitches required to balance or complete the stitch pattern after the repeat or repeats have been worked.

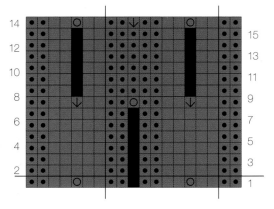

Gauge

The gauge of a piece of knitting is the number of stitches and rows counted over a given measurement. Gauge is controlled by the type of yarn, the size of the needles, and the stitch pattern. Accurate gauge is crucial to a successful result.

Why gauge matters

A knit designer will establish the number of stitches and rows needed to obtain a given measurement—usually 4 inches or 10 centimeters—in the chosen yarn and stitch pattern, and use that information when calculating the size and shape of a garment. However, knitters can afford to be more relaxed about gauge when knitting a scarf, as getting a good fit is not crucial.

Knitting patterns emphasize that you must use the correct yarn, but this does not apply to the needle size. The recommended needle size is a guide only; it does not matter what size needles you use as long as you achieve the correct gauge. The same yarn with a different needle size or type of needle can produce a different-sized swatch. Even your mood or how you hold your needles can change the gauge. It is therefore essential that you knit a swatch and check the gauge before starting on the real thing. It is the only way to save wasting time and effort, creating a knit that either does not fit or is the wrong size.

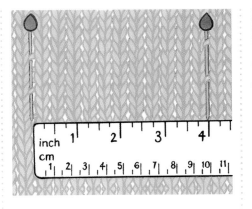

1 Count and mark the stitches with pins, then measure between the pins. If the measurement is correct, you will know that your finished piece will be the right width. If your marked stitches measure less, you are knitting too tightly and the garment will be too narrow. Knit another swatch using larger needles, and measure again. If the marked stitches measure more than they should, you are knitting loosely and the piece will be too wide. Knit another swatch on smaller needles, and measure again.

2 Mark the number of rows and check the measurement. If it is correct, go ahead and start knitting. If the marked rows measure less, your knitting is tight and the piece will be too short. Try using larger needles for your next swatch. If the marked rows measure more, your knitting is loose and the piece will be too long. Try knitting another swatch using smaller needles.

How to measure gauge

Knit a swatch using the required needle size. Always add a few extra stitches and work a few more rows because the edge stitches will be distorted. Check the making-up instructions and, if necessary, press the swatch. Working on a flat surface, use a tape measure or metal ruler to check the gauge.

Blocking and pressing

As part of the finishing process for a scarf, you should block and/or press the knitted piece. By using heat, water, or steam you can even out any stitch irregularities and help curled edges lie flat, so giving your knitting a professional finish.

Steaming and pressing

Knitting worked in natural fibers, such as wool or cotton, and fairly plain textures can usually be steam-pressed—always check your pattern and the yarn label. Pin the piece out to size on a blocking board using the grid on the fabric as a guide (see opposite), then place a clean, dry or damp cloth over the fabric and press lightly with an iron set at the recommended temperature—keep the iron moving and don't leave the full weight of the iron on the fabric. Never place an iron directly on a knitted fabric as you may burn the fibers and spoil the knitting.

Boldly textured fabrics such as cables should not be pressed as this will flatten the pattern. Instead, hold a steam iron over the cloth and allow the steam to pass through to the knitted fabric.

After pressing or steaming, remove the cloth and leave the fabric to dry before removing the knitting from the blocking board.

Ribs can lose their elasticity when pressed, so unless they need to match the width of the rest of the piece, pressing is best avoided.

If you need to join pieces, the seams will need to be pressed. Working on the wrong side, place a dry or damp cloth over the seams and use an iron set at the recommended temperature to lightly press the seams.

Do not press or steam synthetic yarns as the heat and steam will take the "body" out of the yarn, making it limp—use the wet-spray method instead. If in doubt as to how to finish your knitting, use the wet-spray method.

PROTECTING THE WORK
Use a cloth to protect knitted fabrics when ironing—never place an iron directly on the work.

Wet blocking

Use this method for yarn that cannot be pressed, textured or fluffy yarns, and boldly textured stitch patterns. Wet the piece gently by hand in lukewarm water. Carefully lift the knitting out of the water, gently squeezing out the water as you lift—do not lift it out while it is soaking wet as the weight of the water will stretch the knitting. To remove the excess water, lay the knitting on a towel and smooth out flat, then loosely roll up the towel from one end, applying a little pressure.

Unroll the towel and lay the knitting on a blocking board. Using long, rustproof, glass-headed or knitting pins, pin the knitting out to size and shape, using the grid on the fabric as a guide. Leave to dry thoroughly to "set" the fabric. Cable fabrics are best wet-blocked with the right side facing up. This enables you to mold the texture.

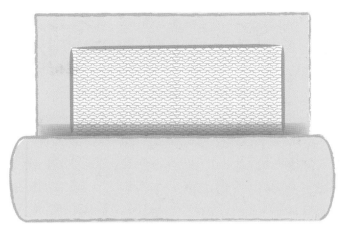

WET BLOCKING
Use the wet-blocking technique for yarns that cannot be pressed.

Spray-blocking

This method is similar to wet blocking and can also be used for yarns that cannot be pressed. Pin the sections of dry knitting out on a blocking board to size and shape, then use a water spray to thoroughly wet the knitting. Press gently with your hands to even out the fabric, then leave to dry before removing the pins.

Three-dimensional blocking

For scarves worked in the round, use steaming, wet- or spray-blocking—choose the method most suited to the yarn and stitch pattern. Work on one side at a time, pinning the knitting out to size, taking care not to damage the stitches. Leave to dry, then repeat on the other side.

If you are blocking a small, circular item, you can drape the piece over an upturned plastic pot or mixing bowl that is the right size. Wet the knitting, drape it over the form, and let dry.

SPRAY BLOCKING
This method is also suited to yarns that cannot be pressed.

MAKING A BLOCKING BOARD
Place a sheet of batting or curtain interlining on a piece of board and cover with gingham fabric. Stretch the fabric without distorting the checks, and secure it on the back with tape or staples. Lay the knitting on the board and match the edges to the checks to ensure they are straight.

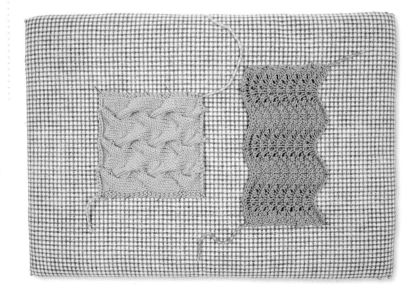

CHAPTER 2

Knit & Purl Stitches

It is amazing that just two stitches—knit and purl—form the basis of every knitted fabric, from familiar patterns like stockinette to more complex textures like basketweave. This chapter demonstrates some of the simpler combinations of these two stitches and goes on to show how they can be used in practice, in a range of beautiful scarves.

Knit and purl stitches step-by-step

Alternate knit and purl stitches to create the simplest textures, group them to make blocks, diagonals, chevrons, and diamonds, or put them together more freely to form motifs. Patterns can be repeated to make an all-over design, or used in panels with simple stitch patterns between. Stitches may also be slipped to increase textural interest.

Moving yarn between the needles

One of the simplest ways of varying the texture of the knitted fabric—as in rib, seed, or moss stitch—is to work a combination of knit and purl stitches along a row, to show not only the V-shape of the knit stitch but the bump of the purl. In order to work one stitch and then the other, the working yarn has to be moved between the needles into the position for the next stitch.

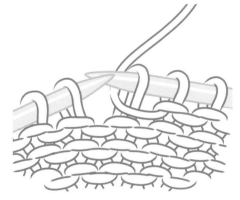

With yarn in back (wyib)
Take the yarn to the back of the right-hand needle, taking care to move it cleanly between the needles and not across the top of the right needle.

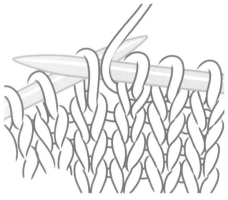

With yarn in front (wyif)
Take the yarn in front of the right-hand needle, taking care to move it cleanly between the needles and not across the top of the right needle.

Slipping a stitch

In some techniques, the knitter may be required to slip a stitch. In most cases this will mean that a stitch needs to be passed from one needle to another. The way that a stitch is slipped will determine the way that it sits on the needle, so it will need to be slipped either "knitwise" or "purlwise."

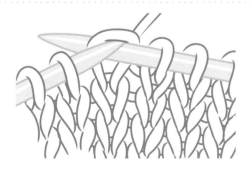

Slip a stitch knitwise
Insert the right needle into the stitch as if to knit and slip from the left needle.

Slip a stitch purlwise
Insert the right needle into the stitch as if to purl and slip from the left needle.

Short row shaping

By working only part of a row and then turning the piece and working back again, one section of the knitting is made longer than the rest. To avoid making a hole where each row is turned, the adjacent stitch is "wrapped." Wrapping may be worked knitwise or purlwise to match the stitch pattern in use.

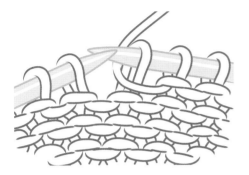

1 Purl the number of stitches required for the short row. The next stitch will be wrapped purlwise. With the yarn at the front, slip the next stitch purlwise. Take the yarn to the back between the needles.

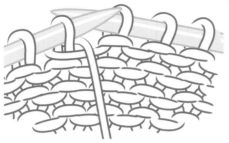

2 Slip the stitch from the right needle onto the left needle. Bring the yarn to the front between the needles. One stitch has been wrapped purlwise. Turn the work. To hide the wrap strands, work up to the first wrapped stitch, insert the right needle under the wrap loop and through the next stitch on the left needle, and knit the two together.

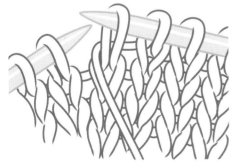

3 Knit the number of stitches required for the short row. With yarn in back of the work, slip the next stitch purlwise. Bring the yarn between the needle tips to the front.

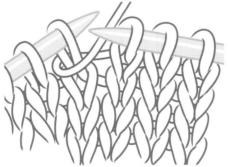

4 Slip the stitch from the right needle back onto the left needle. Take the yarn to the back between the needle tips. One stitch has been wrapped knitwise. Turn the work.

EXAMPLES

From the top: slip stitch on garter stitch ground; short rows; short rows with each segment worked in a different yarn; twisted rib

Wrapping yarn around stitches

Wrapping gathers groups of stitches together to create texture. Stitches are bound by passing a stitch across a given group of stitches. In this mock cable pattern three stitches are bound with one stitch.

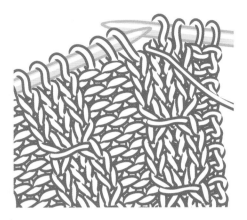

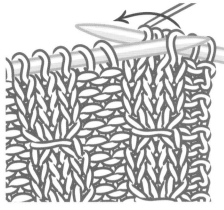

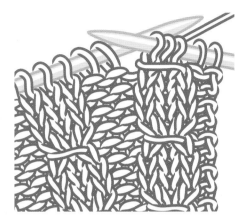

Bind 3 (B3)

1 With the yarn in back, the first stitch of the group is slipped purlwise. The slipped stitch is used to bind the stitches. To compensate for the slipped stitch, an extra stitch needs to be made. Knit the next stitch, then bring the yarn to the front between the needles.

2 Take the yarn from the front across the right needle and to the back. The yarn lying across the right-hand needle makes a yarn-over. Knit the next stitch. Now insert the left-hand needle into the slipped stitch from left to right. Pass the slipped stitch over (psso) the first knitted stitch, the new stitch, and the next knitted stitch.

3 The bind is now completed and the first mock cable has been formed. By binding each group of three stitches, mock cables are formed across the row.

Seed stitch

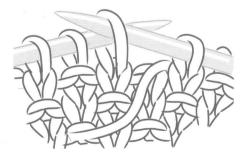

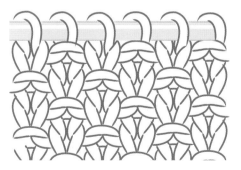

1 Cast on the required number of stitches and hold the needle with the stitches in your left hand. Use the right-hand needle to knit the first stitch, then bring the yarn to the front between the needles, and purl the next stitch.

2 Take the yarn to the back and knit the next stitch. Now purl one stitch, then knit one stitch all the way across the row. Each knit stitch will produce a "V" on the front of the fabric and each purl stitch will create a ridge.

3 On the next row a "V" (knit stitch) is worked over each ridge and a ridge (purl stitch) over each "V." Knit one stitch, then purl one stitch across the row. Continue to work every row in this way to produce a seed stitch fabric.

Rib

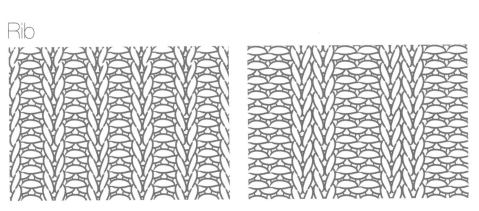

Traditionally, many garments begin with a rib because it keeps the edge of the work tight and can prevent items from becoming misshapen or baggy with use. A rib is created by alternating knit and purl stitches along one row and then, on subsequent rows, matching stitches over the top of each other (so that knit stitches sit on top of knit stitches, and purl on top of purl, and so on). On both sides of the work, the stitches line up to form small ridges. Ribs can be regular, such as single rib (right above) which is made up of one knit stitch then one purl stitch, or double rib, which is knit two, purl two (left above). Or they can be irregular, knit three, purl one, for example.

Extended knit stitches

Extending stitches is another way of adding texture to a knitted fabric.

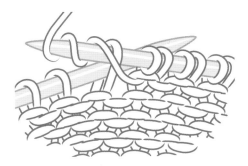 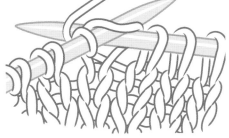

Winding yarn around needle

1 Insert the right-hand needle into the next stitch as if to knit or purl. Wind the yarn around the needle the number of times stated in the pattern and work the stitch.

2 On the subsequent row, work up to an extended stitch, work one stitch into the first wrap, and allow the other wraps to drop off the left-hand needle.

EXAMPLES
From the top: seed stitch; single-stitch rib; four-stitch rib; extended stitch

Knit and Purl Library

All the stitch patterns in this stitch library either make excellent all-over stitch patterns for a scarf or shawl, or could be worked as decorative panels in scarves or shawls of your own design. Patterns that frequently alternate between knit and purl stitches look great in variegated or hand-dyed yarns.

Waffle stitch I

This simple waffle stitch pattern can be used as an all-over stitch pattern or try it as a contrasting panel along the selvage of a scarf.

- **Row 1** (RS) *K1, P1; repeat from * to last st, K1.
- **Row 2** Knit.

These 2 rows form the stitch pattern.

Customize your scarf:
For an attractive variation, substitute this pattern for part or all of Simple but Sublime (page 42).

Basketweave

This intriguing and aptly named pattern is easy to memorize and can either be used as an interesting contrast along an edge or as an all-over pattern.

- **Row 1** (RS) Knit.
- **Row 2** K4, P3, *K5, P3; repeat from * to last 4 sts, K4.
- **Row 3** P4, K3, *P5, K3; repeat to the last 4 sts, P4.
- **Row 4** Repeat row 2.
- **Row 5** Knit.
- **Row 6** P3, *K5, P3; repeat from * to end.
- **Row 7** K3, *P5, K3; repeat from * to end.
- **Row 8** Repeat row 6.

These 8 rows form the stitch pattern.

Customize your scarf:
Substitute this pattern for part or all of St. Alban's Scarf (page 50). Cast on 25 sts and work the first and last 3 sts as described in the scarf pattern.

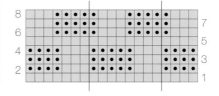

Concentric squares

This stitch pattern makes an excellent edging at the start or end of a scarf. Embellish the center of the squares with embroidery or buttons for extra texture.

- **Row 1** (RS) Knit.
- **Row 2** Purl.
- **Row 3** K2, *P8, K2; repeat from * to end.
- **Row 4** P2, K8, P2; repeat to end.
- **Row 5** K2, *P2, K4, P2, K2; repeat from * to end.
- **Row 6** P2, *K2, P4, K2, P2; repeat from * to end.
- **Repeat** the last 2 rows twice more.
- **Row 11** Repeat row 3.
- **Row 12** Repeat row 4.
These 12 rows form the stitch pattern.

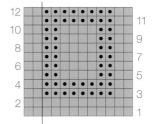

Customize your scarf:

Cast on 45 sts and substitute the eight-stitch square for the five-stitch garter stitch panel of Dropped and Wrapped (page 46).

Zigzag

This pattern is basically a knit-two purl-two rib offset every two rows and makes an interesting all-over stitch pattern for any scarf.

- **Row 1** (RS) *P2, K2; repeat from * to last 2 sts, P2.
- **Row 2** *K2, P2; repeat from * to last 2 sts, K2.
- **Row 3** K1, *P2, K2; repeat from * to last 1 st, P1.
- **Row 4** Repeat the 3rd row.
- **Row 5** *K2, P2; repeat from * to last 2 sts, K2.
- **Row 6** *P2, K2; repeat from * to last 2 sts, P2.
- **Row 7** P1, *K2, P2; repeat from * to last 1 st, K1.
- **Row 8** Repeat row 7.
- **Row 9** Repeat row 1.
- **Row 10** Repeat row 2.
- **Row 11** Repeat row 7.
- **Row 12** Repeat row 7.
- **Row 13** Repeat row 5.
- **Row 14** Repeat row 6.
- **Row 15** Repeat row 3.
- **Row 16** Repeat row 3.
These 12 rows form the pattern.

Customize your scarf:

Diffuse the stripes and substitute this stitch pattern for that of Classic Stripes (page 90).

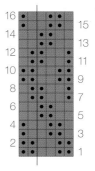

Wrapped stitch rib

When making any of the scarves in this book, a single repeat of this stitch pattern will add interest and show off a yarn's texture and color. To vary the pattern, adjust the number of stitches wrapped, the number of wraps, or the frequency of the wrapped stitches.

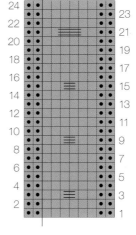

- **Row 1 (RS):** P2, *K6, P2; repeat from * to end
- **Row 2** K2, *P6, K2; repeat from * to end.
- **Row 3** P2, *K2, Wr2, K2, P2; repeat from * to end
- **Row 4** K2, *P6, K2; repeat from * to end.
- **Rows 5–6** Repeat rows 1–2.

Repeat rows 1–6 twice more.

- **Row 19** P2, *K6, P2; repeat from * to end.
- **Row 20** K2, *P6, K2; repeat from * to end.
- **Row 21** P2, *K1, Wr4, K1, P2; repeat from * to end.
- **Row 22** K2, *P6, K2; repeat from * to end.
- **Rows 23–24** Repeat rows 1–2.

These 24 rows form the stitch pattern.

Special abbreviations

Wr2 ▤

Wrap 2 sts: *with the yarn in back, slip 2 sts from the left-hand needle onto the right-hand needle; with the yarn in front, slip 2 sts from the right-hand needle onto the left hand needle; repeat from * twice more; with the yarn in back, slip 2 sts from the left-hand needle onto the right-hand needle.

Wr4 ▤

Wrap 4 sts: *with the yarn in back, slip 4 sts from the left-hand needle onto the right-hand needle; with the yarn in front, slip 4 sts from the right-hand needle onto the left hand needle; repeat from * twice more; with the yarn in back, slip 4 sts from the left-hand needle onto the right-hand needle.

Customize your scarf:

Substitute this stitch pattern for that of Cable and Baubles (page 64).

Drop stitch pattern

The drape of this pattern can be further improved by replacing the yarn-over with a double yarn-over and dropping two stitches a few rows on. The number of rows worked before the dropped stitch may also be altered to vary the pattern.

- **Row 1** (RS) P2, *K2, yo, K2, P4; repeat from * to last 6 sts, K2, yo, K2, P2.
- **Row 2** *K2, *P5, K4; repeat from * to last 7 sts, P5, K2.
- **Row 3** *P2, *K5, P4; repeat from * to last 7 sts, K5, P2.
- **Rows 4–7** Repeat rows 2 and 3 twice more.
- **Row 8** *K2, *P2, drop the next st off the needle an allow it to hang free from either needle, P2, K2, yo, K2; repeat from * to last 7 sts, P2, drop the next st off the needle, P2, K2.
- **Row 9** *P2, *K4, P5; repeat from * to last 6 sts, K4, P2.
- **Row 10** *K2, *P4, K5; repeat from * to last 6 sts, P4, K2.
- **Rows 11–14** Repeat rows 9 and 10 twice more.
- **Row 15** P2, *K2, yo, K2, P2, drop the next st off the needle an allow it to hang free from either needle, P2; repeat from * to last 6 sts, K2, yo, K2, P2.

Rows 2–15 form the pattern.

Note for Drop Stitch Pattern

All the stitches in this swatch were worked through the back of the loops. They can be worked through the front but the stitches on either side of the dropped stitch may become baggy.

Customize your scarf:

Substitute this stitch pattern for part or all of St. Alban's Scarf (page 50).

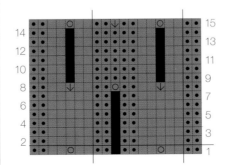

■ *no stitch*

↓ *drop the stitch off the needle*

Waffle stitch II

The right side and the wrong side of this simple stitch pattern look different but both are attractive.

Front

Reverse

- **Row 1** (RS): *P1, K3; repeat from * to last st, P1.
- **Row 2** *K1, P3; repeat from * to last st, K1.
- **Row 3** Repeat row 1.
- **Row 4** Knit.

These 4 rows form the pattern.

Customize your scarf:

Substitute this pattern for that of Simple but Sublime (page 42).

Simple but Sublime

A basic stitch shares the stage with hand-painted fiber, creating a divine knitting experience and a most cherished gift. Easy to create, it's the perfect scarf to get you going, and you can ring the changes by knitting it with a different yarn.

Yarn

Fine yarn (#2), 100% wool, 225 yd (100 m), 4 oz (120 g), I hank; red

Needles & notions

- US 13 (9 mm) knitting needles
- Tapestry needle

Gauge

13 sts equal 4 in (10 cm) in seed stitch

Size

Scarf measures 110 in (279 cm) long, 4 in (10 cm) wide

Making the scarf

Cast on 13 sts.
- **Row 1** *K1, P1, repeat from * to last stitch, K1.
Repeat last row until 110 in (279 cm) long or desired length.
Bind off loosely.
Weave in ends.
Spray-block.
Attach fringe to both ends (see pages 130–131)

Ruched but Not Rushed

Simple stitches, beautiful yarn, easy comfort knitting—that is how I would best describe this project. Combining the brushed suri with the silk alpaca creates a wonderful ruched effect. This project is not to be rushed but you'll enjoy creating every stitch of this beautifully soft, luxury wrap.

Making the scarf

With Yarn A and smaller needle, cast on 299 sts.
Knit 6 rows.

- **Next row** Change to Yarn B and larger needle, K1, *yo, K1, repeat from * across row (598 sts).

Work in reverse stockinette stitch for 4 in (10 cm), beginning P row and ending K row.

- **Next row** P1, *yo, P3tog, repeat from * to end (398 sts).

Change to Yarn A and smaller needles; knit 10 rows.

- **Next row** Change to Yarn B and larger needle, K1, *yo, K1, repeat from * across row (795 sts).

Work in reverse stockinette stitch for 4 in (10 cm) as before.

- **Next row** P1 *yo, P3tog, repeat from * to last 2 sts, yo, P2 (530 sts).
- **Next row** Change to Yarn A and smaller needle, K 10 rows.
- **Next row** Change to Yarn B and larger needle, K1, *yo, K1, repeat from * across row (1059 sts).

Work in reverse stockinette stitch for 4 in (10 cm), as before.

- **Next row** P1 *yo, P3 tog, repeat from * to last 2 sts, yo, P2 (706 sts).

Change to Yarn A and smaller needles; knit 6 rows. Bind off loosely.
Weave in ends.
Spray-block.

Yarn

- Lightweight yarn (#3), 70% alpaca, 30% silk; 1¾ oz (50 g), 91 yd (83 m), 3 skeins (Yarn A)
- Medium-weight yarn (#3), 67% baby suri, 22% merino, 11% bamboo; 1¾ oz (50 g), 142 yd (130 m); 9 hanks (Yarn B)

Needles & notions

- US 6 (4 mm) circular knitting needles
- US 9 (5.5 mm) circular knitting needles
- Tapestry needle

Gauge

- With Yarn B and larger needles, 15 sts equal 4 in (10 cm)

Size

Wrap measures 75 in (191 cm) long, 16 in (40 cm) wide

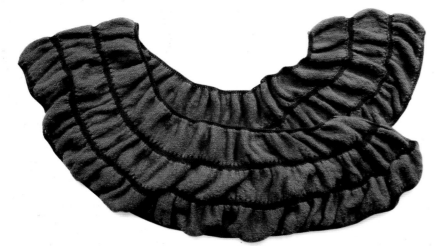

Dropped and Wrapped

This scarf is what happens when you manipulate the knit and purl stitch. It's an easy pattern with just a twist every 16 rows. As an alternative, you could try it with finer yarn and smaller needles and add some beads, and you'll have a showstopper scarf for an evening out on the town.

Making the scarf

With US 8 (5 mm) needles, cast on 33 stitches.

- **Row 1** Knit.
- **Row 2** P2, *K5, P1, K1, P1, repeat from * to last 7 stitches, K5, P2.
- Repeat last two rows 6 more times (14 rows).
- **Row 15** [Kw3] twice, *slip 1, K1, psso, [K1, pso] 3 times, slip last stitch from right-hand needle back to left-hand needle, K2togw3, [Kw3] twice, repeat from * 2 more times, slip 1, K1, psso, [K1, pso] 3 times, slip last stitch from right-hand needle back to left-hand needle, k2togw3, Kw3.
- **Row 16** Purl the second stitch on left-hand needle leaving stitch on left needle, then purl first stitch, pull both off, and drop extra loops (note: stitches will be long and exaggerated), * cast on 5 stitches using easy loop method, purl third stitch on left-hand needle leaving stitch on left needle, knit second stitch, then purl first stitch, pull all off at once and drop extra loops; repeat from * twice more, cast on 5 stitches using easy loop method, purl second stitch on left-hand needle leaving stitch on left needle, then purl first stitch, pull both off, and drop extra loops.

Repeat from row 1–16 until 45 in (114 cm) long, ending with row 14. Bind off loosely. Weave in ends loosely. Spray-block. Add fringe at each end (see pages 130–131).

Yarn
- Worsted-weight yarn (#4); 225 yd (206 m); 1–2 skeins (allowing for fringe)

Needles & notions
- US 8 (5 mm) knitting needles
- Tapestry needle

Gauge
- 19 sts and 26 rows in stitch pattern equal 4 in (10 cm)

Size
- Scarf measures 45 in (114 cm) long, 6 in (15 cm) wide

Special abbreviations
- **Kw3:** When knitting next stitch, wrap yarn 3 times around the right-hand needle, then complete stitch.
- **pso:** Pass previous stitch over.
- **K2togw3:** When knitting next 2 stitches together, wrap yarn 3 times around the right-hand needle, then complete stitch.

The Crown Jewels

Simple loops knit with fine yarns make this scarf a signature wardrobe piece. Yes, it's warm because it's knit with a cashmere and silk blend but I'm sure you'll want to wear it long after the coat and hat come off. Wrap it around twice and it serves as a fiber necklace. Add a family heirloom and you'll be dressed for an evening out!

Yarn

Baby-weight yarn (#2), 70% cashmere, 30% Schappe silk; 328 yd (300 m), 1 oz (25 g); 3 colors, #27 (Yarn A), #29 (Yarn B), (Yarn C) #30, 1 ball of each

Needles & notions

- US 6 (4 mm) circular needles
- Tapestry needle
- Slip ring marker

Gauge

22 sts equal 4 in (10 cm)

Size

Scarf measures 45 in (115 cm) long, 6 in (15 cm) wide

Making the scarf

Work on circular knitting needles throughout.

With Yarn A, cast on 250 sts.

Join into a circle without twisting. Place slip marker on right needle. (Slip marker on every round.)

** K7 rounds, ending at marker. Bind off 225 sts. Break off Yarn A, join in Yarn B, K25. Remove marker. Cast on 225 sts, replace marker on right needle, and join into a circle. **

Repeat from ** to ** 4 more times, changing from Yarn B to Yarn C, Yarn C to Yarn A, Yarn A to Yarn B, and Yarn B to Yarn C.

K7 rounds, ending at marker. Bind off loosely.

Weave in ends.

St. Alban's Scarf

Inspiration can come from many places. This scarf was inspired by a 100-year-old brick building I walk past daily and I wanted to translate the simple yet quietly handsome brickwork into a stitch pattern. This is a perfect project for the new knitter because it uses only knit and purl stitches.

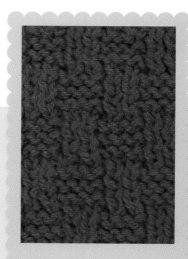

Yarn

Worsted-weight yarn (#4), 100% baby alpaca, 128 yd (117 m), 3½ oz (100 g): 3 skeins

Needles & notions

- US 8 (5 mm) knitting needles or size needed to obtain gauge
- Tapestry needle

Gauge

18 sts and 24 rows in stitch pattern equal 4 in (10 cm) in worsted-weight yarn

Size

Scarf measures 42 in (107 cm) long, 5 in (13 cm) wide

Making the scarf

With yarn doubled, cast on 26 sts.
- **Row 1** Slip 3 purlwise wyib, *K4, K1, P1, K1, P1, repeat from * to last 7 sts, K4, P3.
- **Rows 2–6** As row 1.
- **Row 7** Slip 3 purlwise wyib, *K1, P1, K1, P1, K4, repeat from * to last 7 sts, K1, P1, K1, P4.
- **Rows 8–12** As row 7

Repeat last 12 rows until scarf measures 42 in (107 cm).
Bind off loosely.
Weave in ends and spray-block.

Half Moon Rising

I like versatility in my knitted projects. This shawl can be worn in multiple ways: as a shrug, a bolero, or a simple scarf. The yarn is the key ingredient—it shifts and changes in texture and at the same time in color. With a relatively small amount of wool, you can make an item for your wardrobe that can become a signature accessory.

Making the scarf

Cast on 82 sts.

- **Row 1** * P2, K2, repeat from * to last two stitches, P2.
- **Row 2** * K2, P2, repeat from * to last two stitches, K2.
- Repeat last 2 rows for 3½ in (9 cm).
- **Next row RS** P, start reverse stockinette.
- **Next row** K; continuing in reverse stockinette stitch, work short rows to shape the back as follows:
- **Row 1** P44, w&t.
- **Row 2** K6, w&t.
- **Row 3** P10, w&t.
- **Row 4** K14, w&t.

Continue in pattern, working 4 more sts on each row until all stitches are worked, ending K row. Shawl should measure 9 in (22.5 cm) in the center.

- **Next row** P10, bind off 10 sts, P to last 20 sts, bind off 10 sts, P to end.
- **Next row** K10, cast on 14 stitches, K to next opening, cast on 14 stitches, K10 (90 sts).
- **Right-side row** *P2, K2, repeat from * to last 2 sts, P2.
- **Wrong-side row** *K2, P2, repeat from * to last 2 sts, K2.

Repeat last two rows until scarf measures 16 in (40 cm) at center back. Bind off loosely and weave in ends. Spray-block.

ADAPTABLE DESIGN

This scarf has slits for your arms, or wear it loosely wrapped around your shoulders like the model.

Yarn

Bulky-weight yarn (#5), 100% wool, thick and thin, 125 yd (150 m), 3½ oz (100 g), 2 hanks

Needles & notions

- US 15 (10 mm) circular needles, length 32 in (81 cm)
- Tapestry needle

Gauge

8 sts equal 4 in (10 cm) in reverse stockinette stitch

Size

Shawl measures 41 in (104 cm) long, 16 in (40 cm) wide

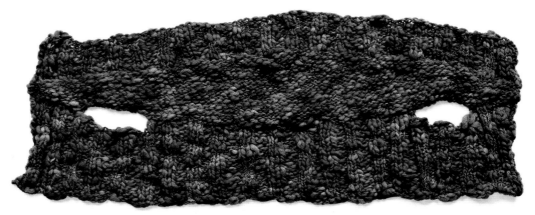

Hubby's Scarf

A scarf for a guy must be masculine as well as soft and comfortable to wear. Here, I chose a traditional herringbone pattern, normally seen in men's suit fabrics, and interpreted it as a knit. The merino/alpaca blend of this yarn hits the spot. It also has nice stitch definition, making it a top choice for simple knit/purl stitch patterns.

Stitch pattern

(Multiple of 10 sts)
- **Row 1** K3, P2, K1, P2, K2.
- **Row 2** P1, K2, P3, K2, P2.
- **Row 3** K1, P2, K5, P2.
- **Row 4** K1, P2, K1, P1, K1, P2, K1, P1.

Making the scarf

Cast on 39 sts.
Set up rows
- **Row 1** K4, work row 3 of stitch pattern to last 5 sts, K2, P3.
- **Row 2** Slip 3 sts purlwise wyib, K1, P1, work row 4 of the stitch pattern to last 4 sts, K1, P3.

Main pattern

- **Row 1** Slip 3 purlwise wyib, K1, work row 1 of stitch pattern to last 5 sts, K2, P3.
- **Row 2** Slip 3 purlwise wyib, K1, P1, work row 2 of stitch pattern to last 4 sts, K1, P3.
- **Row 3** Slip 3 purlwise wyib, K1, work row 3 of stitch pattern to last 5 sts, K2, P3.
- **Row 4** Slip 3 purlwise wyib, K1, P1, row 4 of stitch pattern to last 4 sts, K1, P3.

Repeat last 4 rows until 40 in (100 cm) long. Bind off loosely. Weave in ends and spray-block.

Alternate scarf

- Make this into an infinity scarf by seaming the cast-on and bind-off sections.

Yarn

Medium-weight yarn (#4), 50% merino, 50% alpaca; 100 yd (91 m), 3½ oz (100 g): 4 hanks

Needles & notions

- US 8 (5mm) knitting needles
- Tapestry needle

Gauge

18 sts and 24 rows equal 4 in (10 cm)

Size

Scarf measures 44½ in (113 cm) long, 8½ in (21 cm) wide

Tip

To join a new ball, add new yarn on a wrong-side row before the last 4 sts. Weave in the ends.

Chapter 3

Cables & Knitted Textures

Traditional cables and other knitted textures are among the glories of the knitter's art, relying on form rather than color to give interest to a knitted piece. The pages that follow demonstrate the effects that can be achieved, along with a selection of irresistible scarves to knit.

Cables and textures step-by-step

Cabling involves transferring one, two, or more stitches onto a short, double-pointed needle in order to work them out of sequence. When the cable needle is held in back, the stitches on the right side make a diagonal from left to right. When held in front, the diagonal runs from right to left. Cable stitches can be knitted, purled, or textured.

Cable stitches

Cable four front (C4F)

1 Slip the first two stitches onto a cable needle and hold in front, then knit the next two stitches from the left needle.

Cable four back (C4B)

1 Slip the first two stitches onto a cable needle and hold in back, then knit the next two stitches from the left needle.

Cable six front (C6F/C6L)

Slip 3 stitches purlwise onto the cable needle and hold in front of the work. Knit the next 3 stitches, then knit the 3 stitches from the cable needle.

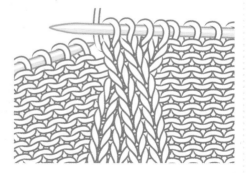

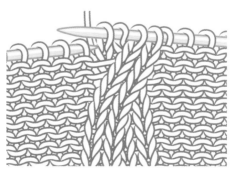

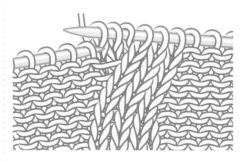

2 Knit the two stitches that are held on the cable needle.

2 Knit the two stitches that are held on the cable needle.

Cable six back (C6B/C6R)

Slip 3 stitches purlwise onto the cable needle and hold in back of the work. Knit the next 3 stitches, and then knit the 3 from the cable needle.

Cable eight front or back (C8F/C8B)

To work this cable, four stitches are held on the cable needle in front of the work. Slip the next four stitches onto a cable needle and leave in front of the work. For a right slant, hold in back.

EXAMPLES

From the top: front four-stitch cable (C4F); six-stitch cable twist to left (C6F); three-stitch twist to left (TW3L); three-stitch twist to left (TW3L) and right (TW3R); bobbles

Twisted cables

Twist 3 back (T3B), moving right

Work to 1 stitch before the knit stitches. Place purl stitch on the cable needle, knit 2 stitches from the left-hand needle, and purl 1 stitch from the cable needle.

Twist 3 front (T4F), moving left

Work to the knit stitches, place 2 knit stitches on the cable needle, purl 1 stitch from the left-hand needle, and knit 2 stitches from the cable needle.

Five-stitch bobble

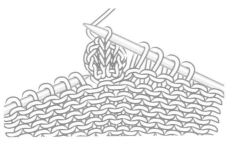

1 Start on a right-side row. Into a stitch, work [K1, yarn over needle] twice, K1, making five stitches on the right needle. Turn and purl the stitches. Turn and knit five stitches.

2 To complete the bobble, turn, P2 together, P1, P2 together, turn, slip 2 knitwise, K1, and pass the slipped stitches over.

Cables and Knitted Textures Library

Cables and knitted textures are more commonly thought of as panels on a relatively plain fabric, and they do work very well as panels, but they also work particularly well along edges—and scarves and shawls have a lot of edge. The weight and robust nature of a cable adds a slight stiffness to an edge that might otherwise fade gracefully into a fabric fold.

Faux cable

This simple, reversible stitch pattern is easy to work and looks good as an all-over stitch pattern or as an edging.

- **Row 1 (RS)** Knit into the front and back of each st.
- **Row 2** P2tog each pair of sts to end.

These 2 rows form the stitch pattern.

Customize your scarf:
Substitute this pattern for part or all of St. Alban's Scarf (page 50).

☑   *Knit into the front and back*

◢   *p2tog*

Honeycomb cable

Worked as an all-over pattern or panel, this reversible pattern provides a focal point for a flower or a button every few rows.

- **Row 1 (RS)** *P4, K8; repeat from * to last 4 sts, P4.
- **Row 2** *K4, P8; repeat from * to last 4 sts, K4.
- **Row 3** *P4, C4B, C4F; repeat from * to last 4 sts, p4.
- **Row 4** Repeat row 2.
- **Rows 5–8** Repeat rows 1 and 2 twice.
- **Row 9** *P4, C4F, C4B; repeat from * to last 4 sts, P4.
- **Row 10** Repeat row 2.

These 10 rows form the stitch pattern.

Customize your scarf:
Substitute this pattern for the fourth cabled section on Galway Blend (page 72).

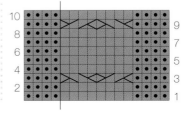

Braided cable

This classic, reversible cable pattern looks good in a panel either toward the center of the scarf or close to an edge. For an easy and simple variation, increase the number of rows worked between the cables.

- **Row 1 (RS)** *P3, K9; repeat from * to last 3 stitches, P3.
- **Row 2** *K3, P9; repeat from * to last 3 stitches, K3.
- **Row 3** *P3, C6F, K3; repeat from * to last 3 stitches, P3.
- **Row 4** Repeat row 2.
- **Rows 5–6** Repeat rows 1 and 2.
- **Row 7** *P3, K3, C6B; repeat from * to last 3 stitches, P3.
- **Row 8** Repeat row 2.
These 8 rows form the stitch pattern.

Customize your scarf:
Substitute for the slim cables pattern in Sugar and Spice (page 68).

Braided cable on stockinette stitch

This approach can be used to soften many of the cable stitch patterns in this book. It offers a more contemporary-looking alternative to more traditional braided cables and can be used as a variation in some of the projects.

- **Row 1 (RS)** Knit.
- **Row 2** Purl.
- **Row 3** K1, *C8F, K4; repeat from last 1 st, K1.
- **Row 4** Repeat row 2.
- **Rows 5–10** Repeat rows 1 and 2 three times.
- **Row 11** K1, *K4, C8F; repeat from * to last 1 st, K1.
- **Row 12** Repeat Row 2.
- **Rows 13–16** Repeat rows 1 and 2 twice.

These 16 rows form the stitch pattern.

Customize your scarf:
Work the center 12 stitches of Lattice cable (page 66) without the reverse stockinette stitch detail.

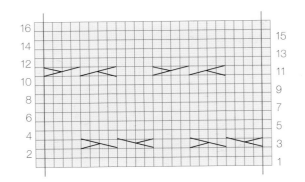

Rib cable on rib

To a knitter this pattern is intriguing as a clear cable motif appears on both sides of the fabric. For the best results, stretch slightly when spray-blocking.

Twists

Back and front crosses produce a subtle change to the fabric which nevertheless changes its visual rhythm. For a more pronounced effect, work through the back loops of the stitch.

Special abbreviations

C8F rib Cable 8 front rib: slip the next 4 sts on the left-hand needle onto a cable needle and hold in front of the work; [K1, P1] twice from the left-hand needle; [K1, P1] twice from the cable needle.

- **Row 1 (RS)** *K1, P1; repeat from * to end.
- **Row 2** Repeat the row 1.
- **Row 3** *[K1, P1] 5 times, C8F rib; repeat from * to last 10 sts, [K1, P1] 5 times.
- **Rows 4–8** *K1, P1; repeat from * to end.

These 8 rows form the stitch pattern.

Customize your scarf:

Work in the center or to one side of Classic Stripes (page 90).

Special abbreviations

FC Front cross: slip 1 onto cable needle and hold in front, P1, K1 from cable needle.

BC Back cross: slip 1 onto cable needle and hold in back, K1, P1 from cable needle

Tw2L Twist 2 left: slip the next st on the left-hand needle onto a cable needle and hold at the front of the work; K1 from the left-hand needle; P1 from the cable needle.

Tw2R Twist 2 right: slip the next st on the left-hand needle onto a cable needle and hold in back of the work; P1 from the left-hand needle; K1 from the cable needle.

- **Row 1 (RS)** *K2, P2; repeat from * to last 2 stitches, K2.
- **Row 2** *P2, K2; repeat from * to last 2 stitches, P2.
- **Row 3** *K2, P1, BC, FC, P1; repeat from * to last 2 stitches, P2.

- **Row 4** *P2, *K1, P1, K2, P1, K1; repeat from * to last 2 stitches, P2.
- **Row 5** *K2, P1, K1, P2, K1, P1; repeat from * to last 2 stitches, K2.
- **Row 6** Repeat row 4.
- **Row 7** *K2, P1, FC, BC, P1; repeat from * to last 2 sts, P2.
- **Row 8** Repeat row 2.

These 8 rows form the stitch pattern.

Customize your scarf:

Work the center 4 sts of the stitch pattern along the edges of Classic Stripes (page 90).

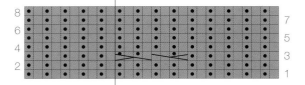

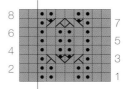

Cable/rib pattern

This makes the perfect all-over stitch pattern for a scarf. It appears to be a rib scarf viewed from one side and a cable scarf from the other. You will need two cable needles.

Front

Reverse

Special abbreviations

C6B rib Cable 6 back rib: slip the next 2 sts on the left-hand needle onto a cable needle and hold in back of the work; slip the next 2 sts on the left-hand needle onto a cable needle and also hold in back of the work; K2 from the left-hand needle; ensure the first cable needle of sts has crossed in front of the second cable needle toward the left, P2 from the second cable needle, K2 from the first cable needle.

C6F rib Cable 6 front rib: slip the next 2 sts on the left-hand needle onto a cable needle and hold in front of the work; slip the next 2 sts on the left-hand needle onto a cable needle and also hold in back of the work; K2 from the left-hand needle; P2 from the second cable needle, K2 from the first cable needle.

- **Row 1 (RS)** *K2, P2; repeat from * to last 2 sts, K2.
- **Row 2** *P2, K2; repeat from * to last 2 sts, P2.
- **Row 3** *[K2, P2] twice, C6B rib, P2, C6F rib; repeat from * to last 8 sts, [P2, K2] twice.
- **Row 4** *P2, K2; repeat from * to last 2 sts, P2.
- **Rows 5–8** Repeat rows 1 and 2 twice.

These 8 rows form the stitch pattern.

Customize your scarf:

Replace the 8 sts that form the C8F in Bobble Wrap (page 76) with the 6 sts of this pattern that hold the cable stitches.

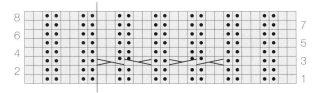

Cables and Baubles

Knit big! The bulky yarn in this scarf makes a grand statement but is also a perfect fiber for your first cable adventure. The cables framed by eyelet lace give you a opportunity to flex your knitting muscles. I included some "baubles" (aka pom-poms), to pump up the fun and add a fashionable touch.

Making the scarf

Cast on 11 sts.
- **Set up row** K5, yo, K1, yo, K5 (13 sts).
- **Row 1** P13.
- **Row 2** K5, yo, slip 1, K2tog, psso, yo, K5.
- **Row 3** As row 1.
- **Row 4** As row 2.
- **Row 5** As row 1.
- **Row 6** K1, C4B, yo, slip 1, K2tog, psso, yo, C4F, K1.

Repeat last 6 rows until scarf measures 73 in (185 cm), ending with row 6.
- **Next row** P3, P2tog, P3, P2tog, P3.

Bind off remaining 11 stitches loosely. Weave in ends. Spray-block.

The pom-poms

Making the pom-poms
- Make 2 large pom-poms, about 4 in (10 cm) across, using both the brushed suri and bulky yarn.
- Make 2 medium pom-poms, about 3 in (7.5 cm) across, using brushed suri.
- Make 2 medium pom-poms, about 3 in (7.5 cm) across, using bulky yarn.

Attaching the pom-poms
Cut 6 x 102 in (260 cm) long strands of the brushed suri yarn. Holding three strands of the yarn together, weave them through the holes made by the yarn-overs. Repeat this for the two rows of yarn-overs. Attach pom-poms as desired to the ends of the strands and the ends of the scarf.

🧶 Yarn
- Super bulky-weight yarn (#6), 100% merino; 45 yd (41 m), 3½ oz (100 g); 4 hanks
- Medium yarn (#3), 67% baby suri, 22% merino, 11% bamboo; 142 yd (130 m); 1¾ oz (50 g); 1 skein

✂ Needles & notions
- US 17 (13 mm) knitting needles
- Cable needle
- Tapestry needle
- Pom-pom maker

📏 Gauge
8 sts and 9 rows equal 4 in (10 cm)

🪜 Size
Scarf measures 96 in (245 cm) long, 5½ in (14 cm) wide from pom-pom to pom-pom

Lattice Cable

Knit in a classic Donegal tweed in a beautiful earthy color, this scarf has classic appeal and will be a hit with any guy—give it as a gift to your favorite man. For a change of pace, try knitting it with a super-soft cashmere or alpaca and see how beautifully the pattern works up on different yarns.

Making the scarf

Cast on 30 sts.

- **Rib row 1** K2, *P2, K2, repeat from * across row.
- **Rib row 2** P2, *K2, P2 repeat from * across row.

Repeat these two rows for 2 in (5 cm), ending rib row 1.

- **(Wrong side) Cable set up row** P2, K1, P4, K2, P4, K4, P4, K2, P4, K1, P2.
- **Row 1** K2, P1, K4, P2, K4, P4, K4, P2, K4, P1, K2.
- **Row 2** P2, K1, P4, K2, P4, K4, P4, K2, P4, K1, P2.

- **Row 3** K2, P1, C4F, P2, C4F, P4, C4F, P2, C4B, P1, K2.
- **Row 4** As row 2.
- **Row 5** K2, P1, K4, P2, C4F, P4, C4F, P2, K4, P1, K2.
- **Row 6** As row 2.
- **Row 7** K2, P1, C4F, P2, K2, T4F, T4B, K2, P2, C4B, P1, K2.
- **Row 8** P2, K1, P4, K2, P2, K2, P4, K2, P2, K2, P4, K1, P2.
- **Row 9** K2, P1, K4, P2, K2, P2, C4F, P2, K2, P2, K4, P1, K2.
- **Row 10** As row 8.
- **Row 11** K2, P1, C4F, P2, K2, P2, K4, P2, K2, P2, C4B, P1, K2.

- **Row 12** As row 8.

Repeat rows 9–12, twice more.

- **Row 21** As row 9.
- **Row 22** As row 8.
- **Row 23** K2, P1, C4F, P2, K2, T4B, T4F, K2, P2, C4B, P1, K2.
- **Row 24** As row 2.

Repeat these 24 pattern rows 20 times or until scarf is desired length. End on row 4 of next pattern.

Work rows 1 and 2 of pattern for 2 in (5 cm).

Bind off loosely in rib.

Weave in ends. Spray-block.

Yarn

Medium-weight worsted yarn (#4), 100% pure new wool, 183 yd (167 m), 3½ oz (100 g); 3 skeins

Needles & notions

- US 8 (5mm) knitting needles
- Cable needle
- Tapestry needle

Gauge

16 sts and 18 rows equal 4 in (10 cm) in cabled pattern

Size

Scarf measures 102 in (260 cm) long, 5½ in (14 cm) wide

Sugar and Spice

In Irish knitting traditions, cables can represent the unbreakable chain of family ties and connections. In each stitch of this shawl, I recall my family's history and all the knitters that came before. But I also wanted to make the shawl modern and ultra-feminine. Interspersing the cables with lace makes it a fashion-forward piece in any wardrobe.

Stitch patterns

Pattern 1: 4-stitch cable (4 sts)
- Row 1 K4.
- Row 2 P4.
- Row 3 C4F.
- Row 4 P4.
- Row 5 K4.
- Row 6 P4.

Repeat these 6 rows.

Pattern 2: Lace-front cable (4 sts)
- Row 1 (RS) K2tog, yo, K2.
- All wrong side rows P.
- Row 3 K2, yo, skpo.
- Row 5 As row 1.

- Row 7 As row 3.
- Row 9 As row 1.
- Row 11 C4F.
- Row 12 P.

Repeat these 12 rows.

Pattern 3: Dropped cable (begins 4 sts)
- Row 1 K2, yo, K2 (5 sts).
- All wrong side rows P.
- Row 3, 5, 7, 9, 11, 13 K5.
- Row 14 Purl.
- Row 15 Slip 2 on to cable needle and hold in front, drop next stitch off left-hand needle, K2, K2 from cable needle (4 sts).

Yarn

Medium-weight yarn (#4), 100% extra-fine merino, 98 yd (100m), 1¾ oz (50 g); 6 balls

Needles & notions

- US 8 (5mm) needles
- Cable needle
- Tapestry needle
- Decorative clasp or closure

Gauge

18 sts equal 4 in (10 cm) in stockinette stitch

Size

Scarf measures 41½ in (105 cm) long, 18 in (46 cm) wide

Special abbreviations

- Sk2togp: Slip 1, K2tog, pass slip st over.
- C8F: Slip 4 sts to cable needle, hold in front, K next 4 sts, K4 from cable needle.
- C8B: Slip 4 sts to cable needle, hold in back, K next 4 sts, K4 from cable needle.

Slim cables

Cabled lace center

Dropped cable (WS)

Lace-front cable (WS)

4-stitch cable (WS)

- **Row 16** P.

Allow dropped sts to unravel to row 1.
Repeat these 16 rows.

Pattern 4: Slim cables (9 sts)

- **Row 1** K9
- **All WS rows** P.
- **Row 3** K9.
- **Row 5** Slip 1 onto cable needle and
  hold in front, K3, K1 from cable needle,
  K1, slip 3 onto cable needle and hold
  in back, K1, K3 from cable needle.
- **Row 6** P.

Repeat these 6 rows.

Pattern 5: Cabled lace center motif (beginning 34 sts)

- **Row 1** K8, yo, skpo, K1, K2tog, yo,
  K8, yo, skp, K1, K2tog, yo, K8.
- **Row 2 and all WS rows** P.
- **Row 3** K9, yo, sk2togp, yo, K10, yo,
  sk2togp, yo, K9.
- **Row 5** C8F, yo, skp, k1, K2tog, yo,
  C8F, yo, skp, K1, K2tog, yo, C8F.
- **Row 7** As Row 3.
- **Row 9** As 1.
- **Row 11** C8f, K1, yo, sk2togp, yo, K1,
  C8F, K1, yo, sk2togp, yo, K1, C8F.
- **Row 13** K1, yo, skp, K1, k2tog, yo, K8,

yo, skp, K1, K2tog, yo, K7, K2tog, yo,
skp, K1, K2tog, yo, K1 (33 sts).
- **Row 15** K2, yo, sk2togp, yo, k10, yo,
  sk2togp, yo, K10, yo, sk2togp, yo, K2.
- **Row 17** K1, yo, skp, K1, K2tog, yo,
  C8B, yo, skp, K1, K2tog, yo, C8B, yo,
  skp, K1, K2tog, yo, K1.
- **Row 19** As Row 15.
- **Row 21** K1, yo, skp, K1, K2tog, yo,
  K8, yo, skp, K1, K2tog, yo, K8, yo,
  skp, K1, K2tog, yo, K1.
- **Row 23** K2, yo, sk2togp, yo, K1, C8B,
  K1, yo, sk2togp, yo, K1, C8B, K1, yo,
  sk2togp, yo, K2.
- **Row 25** K8, yo, skp, K1, k2tog, yo,
  K8, yo, skp, K1, k2tog, yo, K6, M1, K1
  (34 sts).
- **Row 26** P.

Repeat rows 3–26.

Making the scarf

Cast on 90 sts.
- **Rib row 1** K2, * P2, k2 repeat from
  * to end.
- **Rib row 2** P2, *K2, P2, repeat from *
  to end.

Repeat last two rows until shawl

measures 1½ in (4 cm), ending rib row 1.
- **Set up row** P2, K2, P4, K1, P4, K2,
  P9,K2,P34, K2, P9, K2, P4, K1, P4, K2,
  P4.
- **Next row (RS)** Work row 1 of pattern
  1, P2, row 1 of Pattern 2, P1, row 1 of
  Pattern 3, P2, row 1 of Pattern 4, P2,
  row 1 of Pattern 5, P2, row 1 of Pattern
  4, P2, row 1 of Pattern 3, P1, row 1 of
  pattern 2, P2, row 1 of Pattern 1.

Continue in this way working successive
rows of each pattern, repeating rows as
given, with sts between patterns as K on
WS rows and P on RS rows, until shawl
measures 40 in (102 cm), ending with
a suitable WS row.

Repeat rib rows 1 and 2 for 1½ in (4 cm).

Finishing

Bind off in rib as set. Weave in ends and
block.

Galway Blend

Moms are not supposed to have favorites, but I admit this is mine. The scarf has a bit of everything I love to knit. The pattern is a sampler of many stitches. Start with a luscious fiber, then stir in cables, lace, and a generous helping of knitted bobbles, and you have my knitted "Galway blend" recipe.

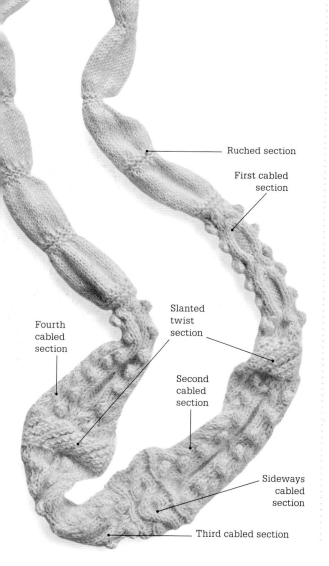

Ruched section

First cabled section

Slanted twist section

Fourth cabled section

Second cabled section

Third cabled section

Sideways cabled section

Special abbreviations

MB (Make bobble)
- **Row 1** [K1, P1, K1, P1, K1] in next stitch, turn.
- **Row 2** K5, turn.
- **Row 3** P5, pass 4th, 3rd, 2nd and 1st sts over 5th st.

T3F Slip next 2 sts to cable needle, hold in front; P next st from left-hand needle; K2 from cable needle.

T3B Slip next st to cable needle, hold in front; K2 from left-hand needle; P1 from cable needle.

RT (Right twist) Skip next stitch and insert needle into 2nd stitch knitwise, draw up a stitch, then insert needle into skipped stitch and knit it, let both stitches fall from needle.

Making the scarf

Using the provisional cast-on method, cast on 22 sts.

Ruched section
- **Rows 1–4** Knit.

Yarn

Lighweight yarn (#3), 60% baby suri alpaca, 40% merino, 164 yd (150 m), 3½ oz (100 g), 3 skeins

Needles & notions
- US 8 (5mm) knitting needles
- Crochet hook
- Cable needle
- Darning needles

Gauge

20 sts equal 4 in (10 cm) in stockinette stitch

Size

Scarf measures 70 in (178 cm) long, 7 in (18 cm) wide

- **Row 5** *Kfb, repeat from * across row (44 sts).
- **Rows 6–23** Work in stockinette stitch starting with a P row and ending with a K row.
- **Row 24** *P2tog, repeat from * across row (22 stitches).
- Repeat rows 1–24 until scarf measures 36 in (91 cm), ending with row 4 (22 sts).

First cabled section

- **Row 1** K1, P1, K4, P1, K1, P1, [Kfb] 4 times, P1, K1, P1, K4, P1, K1 (26 sts).
- **Row 2** P1, K1, P4, K1, P1, K1, P8, K1, P1, K1, P4, K1, P1.
- **Row 3** K1, P1, C4B, P1, MB, P1, C4B, C4F, P1, MB, P1, C4F, P1, K1.
- **Row 4** As row 2.
- **Row 5** K1, P1, K4, P1, K1, P1, K8, P1, K1, P1, K4, P1, K1.
- **Row 6** As row 2.
- **Row 7** K1, P1, C4B, P1, K1, P1, C4B, C4F, P1, K1, P1, CBF, P1, K1.
- **Row 8** P1, K1, P4, K1, P1, K1, P2, K4, P2, K1, P1, K1, P4, K1, P1.
- **Row 9** K1, P1, K4, P1, MB, P1, K2, P4, K2, P1, MB, P1, K4, P1, K1.
- **Row 10** As row 8.
- **Row 11** K1, P1, CFB, P1, K1, P1, K2, P4, K2, P1, K1, P1, C4F, P1, K1.
- **Row 12** As row 8.
- **Row 13** K1, P1, K4, P1, K1, P1, K2, P4, K2, P1, K1, P1, K4, P1, K1.
- **Row 14** As row 8.
- **Row 15** K1, P1, C4B, P1, MB, P1, K2, P4, K2, P1, MB, P1, C4F, P1, K1.
- **Row 16** As row 8.
- **Row 17** K1, P1, K4, P1, K1, P1, C4F, C4B, P1, K1, P1, K4, P1, K1.

- **Row 18** As row 2.

Repeat rows 3–18, then rows 3–7 again.

- **Last row** P1, K1, [P2tog] twice, [K1, P1] twice, [P2tog] 3 times, [P1, K1] twice, [P2tog] twice, K1, P1 (19 sts/40 rows).

Slanted twist section

Note: section worked sideways; last st on every RS row is worked from main body.

Cast on 11 stitches.

- **Row 1** P2, [RT] twice, K2tog, yo, K1, P1, P2tog, turn.
- **Row 2** K2, P7, K2.
- **Row 3** P2, K1, RT, K2tog, yo, RT, P1, P2tog, turn.
- **Row 4** As row 2.
- **Row 5** P2, RT, K2tog, yo, RT, K1, P1, P2tog, turn.
- **Row 6** As row 2.

- **Row 7** P2, K1, K2tog, yo, [RT] twice, P1, P2tog, turn.
- **Row 8** As row 2.
- **Row 9** P2, K2tog, yo, [RT] twice, K1, P1, P2tog, turn.
- **Row 10** As row 2.
- **Row 11** P2, K1, [RT] 3 times; P1, P2tog, turn.
- **Row 12** As row 2.

Repeat rows 1–12 twice more (36 rows). Bind off in K and P as set, purling last 2 sts tog.

Second cabled section

With right side facing, pick up and knit 22 sts.
From side edge of Slanted Twist Section:
- **Row 1** P to end.

Work 40 rows as First Cabled Section (19 sts). Do not bind off.

Sideways cabled section

Note: section worked sideways.
Cast on 13 sts.
- **Row 1 RS** Slip 1, K1, P2, [K2, P2] twice, Skpo, turn.
- **Row 2 WS** P1, [K2, P2] 3 times.
- **Row 3** Slip 1, K1, P2, T3F, T3B, P2, Skpo, turn.
- **Row 4** P1, K3, P4, K3, P2.
- **Row 5** Slip 1, K1, P3, C4F, P3, Skpo, turn.
- **Row 6** As row 4.
- **Row 7** Slip 1, K1, P2, T3B, T3F, P2, Skpo, turn.
- **Row 8** As row 2.
- **Row 9** Slip 1, K1, P1, T3B, P2, T3F, P1, Skpo, turn.
- **Row 10** P1, K1, P2, K4, P2, K1, P2.
- **Row 11** Slip 1, K1, P1, K2, P4, K2 , P1, Skpo, turn.

- **Row 12** As row 10.
- **Row 13** Slip 1, K1, P1, T3F, P2, T3B, Skpo, turn.
- **Row 14** As row 2.

Repeat rows 3–14, then 3–12 again.
Bind off in K and P as set, working last 2 sts as Skpo.

Third cabled section

With right side facing, pick up and knit 22 sts from side edge of sideways cabled section.
- **Row 1** P to end. Work 40 rows as First Cabled Section (19 sts). Do not bind off.

Slanted twist section

Work 36 rows as before.
Bind off as given.

Fourth cabled section

With right side facing, pick up and knit 22 sts from side edge of Slanted Twist Section.
- **Row 1** P to end.

Work 39 rows as First Cabled Section, ending RS row.
- **Last row** P1, K1, P1, K4, P1, K1, P1, [P2tog] 4 times, P1, K1, P1, K4, P1, K1, P1 (22 sts).

Do not bind off.

Finishing

Remove waste yarn at provisional cast-on edge. Using Kitchener stitch, graft the cast-on edge to the last row.
Weave in ends. Block lightly.

CONTRASTING TEXTURES

With less textural detail, the ruched section (right) perfectly offsets the more complex cabled areas.

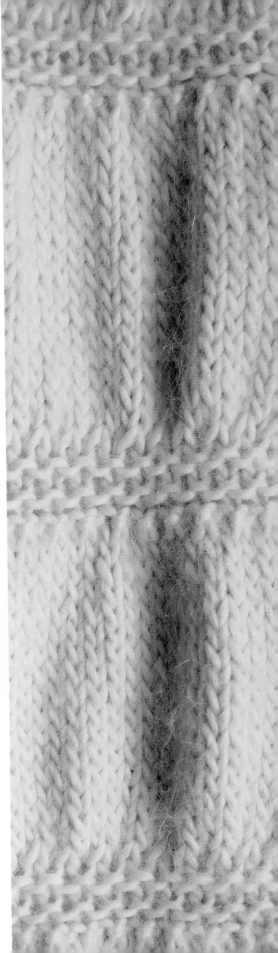

Bobble Wrap

Everything is oversized for this scarf, even its fashion sense. Wear it at least three ways with three different outfits—long as a scarf on a snowy walk; as a shoulder wrap for an evening out; or wrapped twice and tied with a smart bow as a statement piece anytime. Anyway you slice it, you'll be both warm and fashionable this winter!

Yarn

Bulky-weight yarn (#5), 50% organic cotton, 50% merino; 45 yd (31 m), 3½ oz (100g); 5 hanks

Needles & notions

- US 13 (10mm) knitting needles
- 3 yd (2.7 m) of 1½ in (2.5cm) wide satin ribbon
- Cable needle
- Tapestry needle

Gauge

10 sts and 12 rows equal 4 in (10 cm)

Size

Scarf measures 63 in (160 cm) long, 9 in (23 cm) wide

Special abbreviations

Bobble

MB = Make bobble

This is worked on one stitch:

- **Row 1** [K1, P1, K1, P1, K1] in next stitch, turn.
- **Row 2** Knit 5, turn.
- **Row 3** Pass 4th, 3rd, 2nd and 1st sts over 5th st.

Cable

C8F Slip 4 sts from left hand needle onto cable needle and hold in front; knit next 4 sts from left-hand needle; knit 4 from cable needle.

Making the scarf

Cast on 27 sts.

- **Row 1** K15, yo, P2tog, [K2, P2] twice, K2.
- **Row 2** P2, [K2, P2] twice, K2, P15.
- **Row 3** As row 1.
- **Row 4** As row 2.
- **Row 5** As row 1.
- **Row 6** P10, K17.
- **Row 7** P15, yo, P2tog, K6, MB, K3.
- **Row 8** As row 6.
- **Row 9** P15, yo, P2tog, K10.
- **Row 10** P10, K2, P15.
- **Row 11** K15, yo, P2tog, K1, C8F, K1.
- **Row 12** As row 10.
- **Row 13** K15, yo, P2tog, K10.in.

Repeat rows 6–13 until scarf measures 59 in (150 cm).

Work rows 6–9 again.

Work row 2 again.

Repeat rows 1 and 2 twice more.

Bind off loosely in K and P as set.

Weave in ends and block lightly.

Weave ribbon through yos, leaving 9 in (23 cm) on each end.

Cowl

I love cowls—they are smaller than a scarf but just as beautiful as their big sister, the shawl. This cowl is meant to fit around the neck to ward off the chill without overpowering the wearer. A quick knit to match a new coat or give as a special gift to a new friend, this cowl will soon become your favorite too.

Making the scarf

Cast on 90 sts and join into a circle without twisting.

- **Rib round** *K3, P2 repeat from *to end.

Repeat last round until cowl measures 1 in (2.5 cm).

Set round P2, K1, P4, K1, P4, K1, P2.

- **Round 1** P2, slip 1 wyib, P4, slip 1 wyib, P4, slip 1 wyib, P2.
- **Round 2** P2, FC, P3, K1, P3, BC, P2.
- **Round 3** P3, slip 1 wyib, P3, slip 1 wyib, P3, slip 1 wyib, P3.
- **Round 4** P3, FC, P2, K1, P2, BC, P3.
- **Round 5** P4, slip 1 wyib, P2, slip 1 wyib, P2, slip 1 wyib, P4.
- **Round 6** P4, FC, P1, K1, P1, BC, P4.
- **Round 7** P5, slip 1 wyib, P1, slip 1 wyib, P1, slip 1 wyib, P5.
- **Round 8** P5, FC, K1, BC, P5.
- **Round 9** P6, slip 3 wyib, P6.
- **Round 10** P6, slip 1 onto cable needle, hold in front, knit second stitch on left needle, then knit first stitch on left needle, knit 1 from cable needle, P6.
- **Round 11** As round 9.
- **Round 12** P5, BC, K1, FC, P5.
- **Round 13** As round 7.
- **Round 14** P4, BC, P1, K1, P1, FC, P4.
- **Round 15** As round 5.
- **Round 16** P3, BC, P2, K1, P2, FC, P3.
- **Round 17** As round 3.
- **Round 18** P2, BC, P3, K1, P3, FC, P2.

Repeat rounds 1–18 once more.
Repeat Rib Round for 1 in (2.5 cm).
Bind off loosely. Weave in ends. Block.

Yarn

Worsted-weight yarn (#4), 100% wool, 230 yd (200 m), 3½ oz (100 g), 1 ball

Needles & notions

- US 8 (5 mm) circular knitting needle
- Cable needle
- Tapestry needle

Gauge

16 sts equal 4 in (10 cm)

Size

Scarf measures 20 in (51 cm) in diameter, 7 in (17.5 cm) wide

Special abbreviations

- **BC:** Back cross. Sl 1 onto cable needle and hold in back, K1, P1 from cable needle.
- **FC:** Front cross. Sl 1 onto cable needle and hold in front, P1, K1 from cable needle.

Knitted Bib

A scarf doesn't always have to be big fluffy and warm—this knitted piece could be worn in both summer and winter. The selection of beaded yarn sets the stage for a beautiful modern knitted necklace. Using non-knitting with knitted stitches, the yarn is manipulated and, with an alchemist's touch, transformed into *faux d'or*—gold.

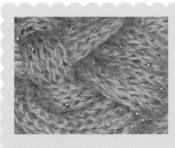

Yarn

Superfine yarn (#1), 74% silk, 26% kid mohair with glass beads; 114 yd (104 m), 1¾ oz (50 g), 1 skein; gold

Needles & notions

- US6 (4 mm) double-pointed needles
- Tapestry needle

Gauge

20 sts equal 4 in (10 cm) in stockinette stitch

Size

- 36 in (90 cm) long, 3 in (7.6 cm) wide

Stitch pattern

To knit I-cord:

- **Step 1** Using double-pointed needles, cast on 5 sts. Do not turn.
- **Step 2** Place needle with 5 sts in left hand. Looking at the right side, push these 5 sts along needle so that the first stitch you cast on is ready to knit and the yarn is attached to the fifth stitch.
- **Step 3** Pull yarn across back and knit 5 sts. Do not turn.
- **Step 4** Hold needle with sts in left hand. Push sts along needle to the right, with yarn on the left.

Repeat steps 2 and 3 until desired length. Bind off.

Making the bib

- Cast on 5 sts and knit a 5 ft (1.5 m) I-cord. Make 2.
- Follow instructions in diagrams for making a carrick knot.
- Sew cast-on edges to bound-off edges.
- Secure threads on wrong side.

CONSTRUCTING THE BIB

1 Different colors have been used for clarity. Fold both I-cords in half. Place looped cord 2 (red) over cord 1 (orange).

2 Take cord 1 (orange) over and under cord 2 (red).

3 Weave cord 1 over and under both I-cords as shown. Gently pull on the I-cords to tighten the knot, while keeping it flat.

4 Draw the ends of the I-cords through the loops you have made.

5 Gently pull on the I-cords for a neat finish, taking care to keep the knot flat. This kind of knot is known as a carrick knot.

CHAPTER 4

Colorwork

One of the greatest pleasures of working with
yarns is their glorious color, whether subtle,
earthy tones or jewel-bright brilliants.
This chapter shows how to incorporate
different colors into your work and produce
stunning scarves, using the simplest stripes
or classic, time-honored Fair Isle.

Colorwork step-by-step

Intarsia involves working blocks of color with separate balls of yarn that are linked together at each color change. In stranded color knitting, pattern rows of frequently changing colors are worked by carrying strands of yarn along the reverse of the work. Fair Isle style knitting uses yarn stranding but only two colors in each row.

Taking color up an edge

Knitting stripes is one of the easiest ways to add color to your design. If each stripe in the sequence has an even number of rows, you can carry the colors up the side edge of the knitting because each color will start and finish on the same edge.

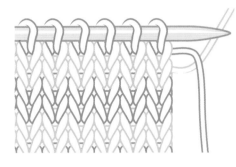

Carrying color up two rows
To carry a color up the side edge of just two rows, bring the new color up behind the old color to begin the next stripe. This makes a neat edge with the carried loops at the back of the work.

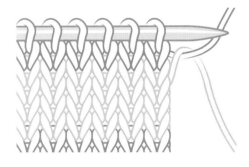

Carrying color up four rows
To carry a color up the side edge of four or more rows, twist the colors at the side edge on every other row to prevent large, loose loops.

Stranding

In this technique, a yarn not in use is carried loosely across the back of the work and, when required, is picked up and passed either underneath or over the other yarn to work the next stitch. This creates a neat pattern of parallel strands on the reverse of the fabric. It is best to leave no more than five stitches between a change in color, since the yarn can create loops on the reverse of the fabric and get caught or snagged. Stranding can be done with one or two hands.

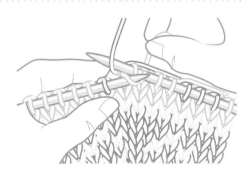

One-handed stranding, right side
1 On a RS (knit) row, knit the required number of stitches in the first color. Drop the yarn, pick up second color, carry it over the dropped yarn, and knit the required stitches. Drop the second color.

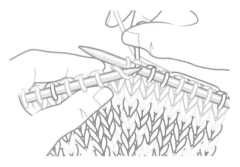

2 Pick up the first color from underneath the second and bring it across the back of the last knitted stitches. Knit the required number of stitches, being careful not to pull the yarn too tightly.

Fair Isle weaving

If a color needs to be carried across the back of the work over more than five stitches, it will need to be caught or woven in. As with stranding, weaving can be done using either the one-handed or two-handed method.

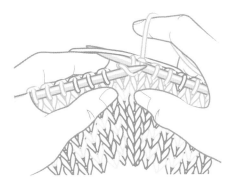
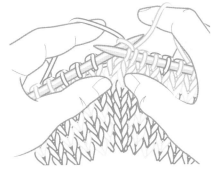

One-handed weaving, right side

1 Work to the point where the second color needs to be caught in. Bring the second color up from under the one in use and over the right needle from right to left.

2 Knit the stitch using the right needle, dropping the stitch and the carried yarn from the left needle as you do so.

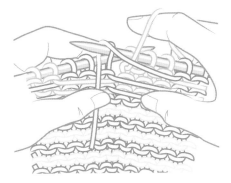
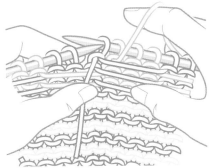

One-handed weaving, wrong side

1 Work to the point where the second color needs to be caught in. Bring the second color up from under the one in use and around the right needle from right to left, anchoring it loosely in place with your left thumb at the front of the work.

2 Using the working yarn, work the next stitch taking care not to take the carried color through the stitch.

EXAMPLES

From the top: repeat Fair Isle motif on striped ground; striped Fair Isle motif on single-color ground; modern Fair Isle motif; garter stitch stripe; stockinette stitch stripe.

Colorwork Library

Adding color to a project should always be a design decision but it could also be a practical one. Adding a color border or panel is a useful way of extending a quantity of yarn, and could coordinate a scarf to a favorite outfit. Each of these stitch patterns can introduce color to a project or could be used as an all-over stitch pattern in a scarf of your own design.

Moss stitch stripe

This stitch pattern is perfect for extending a limited supply of yarn. Combine the project yarn with a second or third yarn to create contrasting ends or panels along a scarf.

Slip stitch pattern

Slip stitch patterns are a great alternative to stranded knitting. It is possible to get the appearance of a Fair Isle while still working rows in a single color.

Stripe sequence

Pink: 2 rows.
Pale pink: 2 rows.
Blue: 2 rows.
Repeat this color sequence and at the same time work the following stitch pattern.

- **Row 1 (RS)** Using a new yarn; *K1, P1; repeat from * to last 1 st, K1.
- **Row 2** *P1, K1; repeat from * to last 1 st, P1.
- **Row 3** Using a new yarn, *P1, K1; repeat from * to last 1 st, P1.
- **Row 4** *K1, P1; repeat from * to last 1 st, K1.
These 4 rows form the stitch pattern.

Customize your scarf:

Substitute the rib pattern used in Classic Stripes (page 90).

Stripe sequence

Start with row 2.
Pink: 2 rows.
Blue: 2 rows.
Repeat this color sequence and at the same time work the following stitch pattern.

- **Row 1 (RS)** Purl.
- **Row 2** Using a new yarn; *K3, wyib slip 1; repeat from * to last 3 sts, K3.
- **Row 3** Purl.
- **Row 4** Using a new yarn; K1, *wyib slip 1, K3; repeat from * to last 2 sts, wyib slip 1, K1.
- **Row 5** Purl.
Rows 2–5 form the stitch pattern.

Customize your scarf:

Substitute Fair Isle pattern in Prince Charming (page 92).

⬜ *Slip 1 st with the yarn in back*

Stockinette and reverse stockinette stitch stripe

This is a simple pattern but its rewards are great. The raised texture, the glimpses of hidden color, and its exuberant bounce makes this a stitch pattern to return to again and again. Try working it with the addition of short rows or using oddments of yarn.

Stripe sequence 2

Stripe sequence 1

Stripe sequence 1

Pink: 6 rows.

Pale pink: 6 rows

Blue: 6 rows.

Repeat this color sequence and at the same time work the following stitch pattern.

- **Row 1 (RS)** Using a new yarn, knit.
- **Row 2** Knit.
- **Row 3** Purl.
- **Row 4** Knit.
- **Row 5** Purl
- **Row 6** Knit.
- **Row 7** Using a new yarn, knit.
- **Row 8** Purl.
- **Row 9** Knit.
- **Row 10** Purl
- **Row 11** Knit
- **Row 12** Purl.

These 12 rows form the stitch pattern.

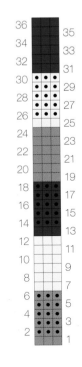

Stripe sequence 2

Pink: 4 rows.

Pale pink: 4 rows.

Blue: 4 rows.

Repeat this color sequence and at the same time work the following stitch pattern.

- **Row 1 (RS)** Using a new yarn, knit.
- **Row 2** Knit.
- **Row 3** Purl.
- **Row 4** Knit.
- **Row 5** Using a new yarn, knit.
- **Row 6** Purl.
- **Row 7** Knit.
- **Row 8** Purl

These 8 rows form the stitch pattern.

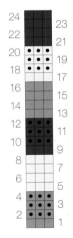

Customize your scarf:

Use as an end-panel on any two-ended scarf knitted in a fairly solid fabric.

Chevron

This stitch pattern is created by working complete rows of a single color. It is perfect for using up oddments of yarn because it responds well to stripes of varying depth and makes the perfect edging for all fabric weights.

Stripe sequence

Pink: 4 rows.

Blue: 8 rows.

Repeat this color sequence and at the same time work the following stitch pattern.

- **Row 1 (RS)** Using a new yarn, *K2tog, K2, [K into the front and back of the next st] twice, K3, slip 1 st, K1, psso; repeat from * to end.
- **Row 2** Knit.
- **Row 3** Knit.
- **Row 4** Knit.
- **Row 5** Using a new yarn, *K2tog, K2, [K into the front and back of the next st] twice, K3, slip 1 st, K1, psso; repeat from * to end.
- **Row 6** Purl.

- **Rows 7–12** Repeat rows 5 and 6 three times.

These 12 rows form the pattern.

Customize your scarf:

Substitute Lace Pattern 2 edging on Lace Triangle Shawl (page 118).

V Knit into the front and back

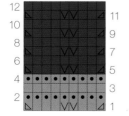

Boxes

The reverse of a Fair Isle motif can be equally as beguiling as the side with the motif. There is something intriguing about seeing the workings of a piece of machinery or even a knitted fabric—so keep it neat and celebrate the Fair Isle strands.

Color codes

Pink = A

Pale pink = B

Blue = C

- **Row 1 (RS)** Using A, knit.
- **Row 2** Using A, purl.
- **Row 3** *K1B, K5A; repeat from * to end.
- **Row 4** *P4A, P2B; repeat from * to end.
- **Row 5** *K3B, K3A; repeat from * to end.
- **Row 6** *P3C, P3B; repeat from * to end.
- **Row 7** *K3B, K3C; repeat from * to end.
- **Row 8** Repeat row 6.

These 8 rows form the pattern.

Customize your scarf:

Substitute Fair Isle pattern used in Two-sided Color Motif (page 96).

Two-sided Fair Isle

The yarn strands of Fair Isle have been used to blend the two yarn colors. Any Fair Isle pattern with an odd number of rows can be worked in the same way and used to substitute a stitch pattern in another scarf.

Color codes
Pale pink = A
Blue = B

- **Row 1 (RS)** *K3A, K3B; repeat from * to last 3 sts, K3A.
- **Row 2** P2B, *P3B, P3A; repeat from * to last 1 st, P1B.
- **Row 3** K2B, *K3A, K3B; repeat from * to last 1 st, K1A.
- **Row 4** *P3B, P3A; repeat from * to last 3 sts, P3B.
- **Row 5** K1A, *K3B, K3A; repeat from * to last 2 sts, K3B.
- **Row 6** P1B *P3A, P3B; repeat from * to last 2 sts, P2A.
- **Row 7** *K3A, K3B; repeat from * to last 3 sts, K3A. These 7 rows form the stitch pattern.

Customize your scarf:
Substitute Fair Isle pattern used in Prince Charming (page 92).

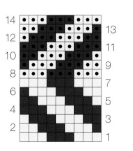

Tiny slip stitch chevron

Worked on larger needles, this stich pattern is a useful substitute for any short repeat solid fabric all-over stitch pattern or as panel detail in a more complex design.

Front

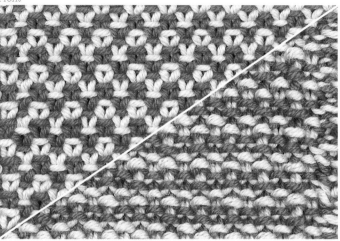

Back

Stripe sequence
Pink: 2 rows.
Pale pink: 2 rows.
Repeat this color sequence and at the same time work the following stitch pattern.

- **Row 1 (RS)** Using a new yarn, *K1, wyif slip 1; repeat from * to last 1 st, K1.
- **Row 2** P2, *wyif of work, slip 1, P1; repeat from *to last 1 sts, P1.

These 2 rows form the stitch pattern.

⊟ *Slip 1 st with the yarn in front*

Customize your scarf:
Substitute the stitch pattern in Simple But Sublime (page 42) or work as a panel in Galway Blend (page 72).

Classic Stripes

The striped scarf never goes out of fashion and is a great addition to a collection of accessories. Mix and match colors around the color wheel and make a striped scarf for every day to match any outfit. Knit in a ribbed stitch means that this one is reversible. Yes, you may have a few extra ends to weave in but we all must suffer for our art.

Yarn

- Lightweight yarn (#3), 100% baby alpaca; 110 yd (100 m). 1¾ oz (50 g): ¾ ball
- 2 hanks main color: cornflower blue
- 2 hanks color B: chocolate brown
- 1 hank color C: pale pink
- 1 hank color D: tan

Needles & notions

- US 4 (3.5 mm) knitting needles
- Tapestry needle
- Row counter

Gauge

28 sts equal 4 in (10 cm) in ribbed pattern

Size

Scarf measures 63 in (160 cm) long, 4 in (10 cm) wide

Ribbed pattern

- **Right-side rows** *K1, P1, repeat from * to last stitch, K1.
- **Wrong-side rows** *P1, K1, repeat from * to last stitch, P1.

Making the scarf

Cast on 35 stitches with main color. Work in ribbed pattern throughout.
** Work 8 rows.
- Change to color B; work 8 rows.
- Change to color C; work 2 rows.
- Change to main color; work 12 rows.
- Change to color D; work 2 rows.
- Change to color C; work 4 rows.
- Change to color B; work 8 rows.
- Change to color C; work 4 rows.
- Change to color D; work 2 rows.
- Change to main color. **

Repeat from ** to ** 9 more times, ending 2 rows color D.
Bind off loosely.
Weave in all ends. Block.

Variation

For your favorite brother, here is a fun color combination:
Main color: deep purple
- **Color B:** dark brown
- **Color C:** mustard
- **Color D:** slate blue

For your fashionable but miminalist best friend, go neutral with a twist:
- **Main color:** natural white
- **Color B:** light gray
- **Color C:** mustard
- **Color D:** dark brown

Prince Charming

Fair Isle knitting originated in the Shetland Islands, Scotland, and became popular when the Prince of Wales (later Edward VIII) wore Fair Isle vests in public in 1921. The technique involves knitting with multiple colors in a single row. Knit in luscious merino and alpaca, this scarf uses traditional Fair Isle patterns of stars and snowflakes.

Yarn

DK weight yarn (#3), 60% baby suri, 40% fine merino, 164 yd (100 m), 3½ oz (100 g); 2 skeins beige; 1 skein each of dark brown, dark red, white

Needles & notions

- US 8 (5mm) knitting needle
- Darning needle
- Row counter

Gauge

20 sts equal 4 in (10 cm) in stockinette stitch pattern

Size

Scarf measures 75 in (190 cm) long, 5½ in (14 cm) wide

Tip

Pattern is worked using Fair Isle techniques, carrying the unused color across the row. You need to weave the carried yarn only if there are more than 5 stitches between color changes.

Waffle stitch pattern

- **RS rows** Slip 3 purlwise wyib, K to last 3 sts, P3.
- **WS rows** Slip 3 purlwise wyib, K1, * P1, K1, rep from * to last 3 sts, P3.

Garter stitch pattern

- **Starting on a RS row** Slip 3 purlwise wyib, K to last 3 sts, P3.
Rep this row 5 more times.
- **Starting on a WS row** Slip 3 purlwise wyib, P to end.
Rep this row 5 more times.

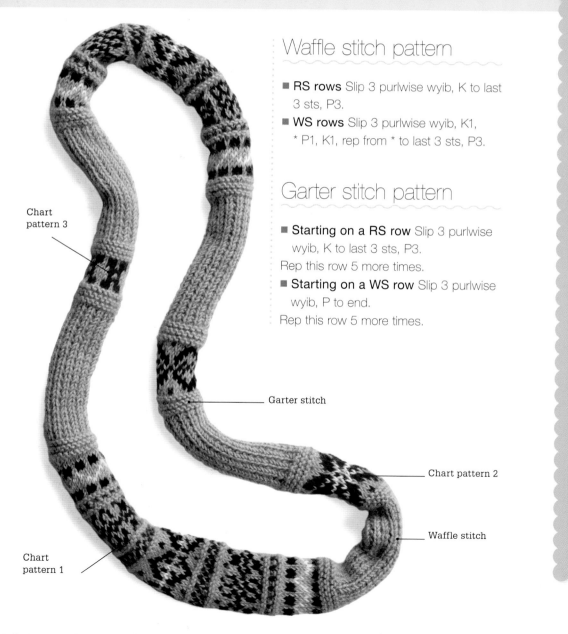

Chart pattern 3

Garter stitch

Chart pattern 2

Waffle stitch

Chart pattern 1

Chart pattern 1

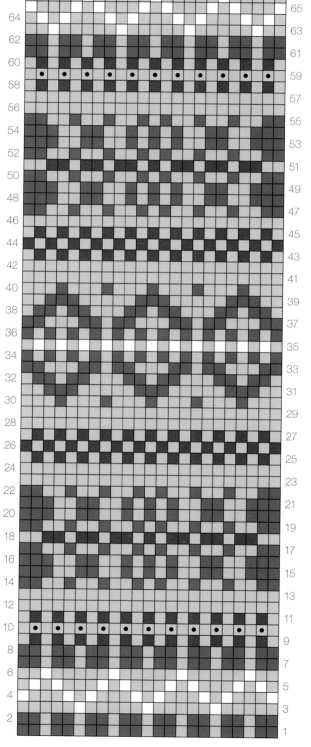

Colorwork panels

Joining in colors as required, work in stockinette (except for Chart Pattern 1, rows 10 and 59, where some sts are worked in reverse stockinette—P on RS rows, K on WS rows).

Panels may begin with either a RS or WS row:

- **RS rows** Slip 3 purlwise wyib, K 23 sts from required chart row reading right to left, change to main color, P3.
- **WS rows** Slip 3 purlwise wyib, P 23 sts from required chart row reading left to right, change to main color, P3.

Making the scarf

Using provisional cast on and main color, cast on 29 sts.

- **Row 1** Slip 3 purlwise wyib, K to last 3 sts, P3.

Work rows 1–68 of Chart Pattern 1, beginning WS row and ending RS row.

Change to main color only.

Work 6 rows garter stitch, beginning WS row.

Work 38 rows waffle stitch, beginning WS row and ending RS row.

Work 6 rows garter stitch, beginning WS row.

Work rows 1–15 of Chart Pattern 2, beginning and ending WS row.

Change to main color only.

Work 6 rows garter stitch, beginning RS row.

Work 38 rows waffle stitch, beginning RS row and ending WS row.

Work 6 rows garter stitch, beginning RS row.

Work rows 30–40 of Chart Pattern 1, beginning and ending RS row.

Change to main color only.

Work 6 rows garter stitch, beginning WS row.

Work 38 rows waffle stitch, beginning WS row and ending RS row.

Work 6 rows garter stitch, beginning WS row.

Work rows 1–68 of Chart Pattern 1, beginning WS row and ending RS row.

Change to main color only.

Work 6 rows of garter stitch, beginning WS row.

Work 38 rows of waffle stitch, beginning WS row and ending RS row.

Work 6 rows of garter stitch, beginning WS row.

Work rows 1–7 of Chart Pattern 3, beginning and ending WS row.

Change to main color only.

Work 6 rows of garter stitch, beginning RS row.

Work 38 rows of waffle stitch, beginning RS row and ending WS row.

Work 6 rows of garter stitch, beginning RS row.

Finishing

Undo provisional cast on. Using Kitchener stitch, graft final row to cast-on row.

Weave in all ends.

Spray-block.

Chart pattern 2

- ☐ beige
- ■ dark brown
- ■ dark red
- ☐ white
- ⊡ reverse stockinette
  (P on RS row, K on WS row)

Chart pattern 3

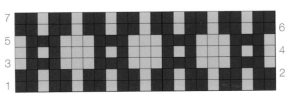

Two-sided Color Motif

This cowl is doubly fantastic because it is in fact doubled! Fully reversible, interchangeable, and multi-purpose are just a few of the adjectives that come to mind. Using similar-weight yarns for the different parts, it's first worked in a diamond pattern for one side, then again in a Fair Isle version of the pattern for the other side.

Making the cowl

Side 1

With US 10 needles and main color, cast on 96 stitches using a provisional cast-on method, place marker and join into a round, taking care not to twist sts. Slip marker on every round.

- **Round 1** *P1, K5, repeat from* across round.
- **Round 2** As round 1.
- **Round 3** *K1, P1, K3, P1, repeat across round.
- **Round 4** As round 3.
- **Round 5** *K2, P1, K1, P1, K1, repeat across round.
- **Round 6** As round 5.
- **Round 7** *K3, P1, K2, repeat across round.
- **Round 8** As round 7.
- **Round 9** As round 5.
- **Round 10** As round 5.
- **Round 11** As round 3.
- **Round 12** As round 3.

Repeat rounds 1–12 until piece measures 8 in (20 cm). Leave all stitches on holder.

Yarn

Aran-weight yarn (#4), 50% royal alpaca, 50% merino, 100yd (91 m), 3½ oz (100 g); main color cherry pink: 2 balls/hanks; color B mulberry: 1 ball/hank; color C midnight blue: 1 ball/hank

✕ Needles & notions

- US 10 (6 mm) 16 in (40 cm) circular knitting needle
- US 10.75 (7 mm) 16 in (40 cm) circular knitting needle
- Stitch marker
- Tapestry needle

Gauge

20 sts equal 4 in (10 cm) in stockinette stitch

Size

Cowl measures 24 in (60 cm) in diameter, 8 in (20 cm) wide

Chart pattern 1

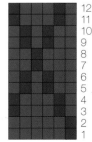

Color B (mulberry)

Color C (midnight blue)

Side 2

Undo cast-on edge. With US 10.75 needles, pick up 96 sts with color B, place marker, join round.

Read all chart rows from right to left, and K all rounds.

■ **Next round** K 6 sts from row 1 of chart 1. Repeat these 6 sts all around.

Work chart rows 2–8 in the same way. Change to US 10 needle and work chart rows 9–12.

Work rows 1–3 of chart 2.

Work 12 rows of chart 1, 3 rows of chart 2, and 12 rows of chart 1.

Finishing

Fold colorwork side inside and use color B to Kitchener-stitch last row of Side 1 to Side 2 to close.

Weave in ends. Block.

Chart pattern 2

■ *Main color (cherry pink)*

■ *Color C (midnight blue)*

REVERSIBLE PIECE
This clever cowl can be worn two ways to go with different outfits—with the patterned side out (right) or the plain side (bottom right).

Brioche à tête

Brioche stitch is a tasty option for any knitter—a bit of a challenge to make but worth the added effort. When selecting colors be sure to go for high contrast to maximize the stitch effect. Knit in bulky yarn, this is a perfect first Brioche recipe. Whip up another using lighter yarn for an airier version of this cowl.

🧶 Yarn

Super bulky yarn (#6), 50% alpaca, 50% wool, 45 yd (41 m), 3½ oz (100 g), 2 skeins main color: olive; 1 skein color B: cream; 1 skein color C: gray

✕ Needles & notions

- US 15 (10 mm) circular needles, length 20 in (51 cm)
- Tapestry needle

📏 Gauge

5 sts equal 4 in (10 cm) brioche stitch pattern

Size

Scarf measures 35 in (89 cm) in diameter, 9 in (23 cm) wide

Making the scarf

With main color, cast on 44 sts.
Do not join.

- **Row 1** Start with your first cast-on stitch (it looks as if you are joining but since you are entering a new color it is not joined yet). With color B, * yo, slip 1 purlwise, bring yarn to front between needles, P1, repeat from * to end (66 sts).

Now join with main color A.

- **Round 2** Using main color, * wyib K2tog (the yo with the following st in color A), wyif slip 1 purlwise (the st in color B), yo, repeat from * to end.

- **Round 3** Using color B * yo, wyib slip 1 purlwise (the st in color A), P2tog (the yo with the followin st in color B), repeat from * to end.

Take yarn to back between needles.

- Repeat rounds 2 and 3 eight more times.
- **Join color C,** repeat round 2.
- **With main color A,** repeat round 3.
- **With main color A,** repeat round 2.
- **With color C,** repeat round 3.

Repeat last 4 rounds once more.

- **With main color A,** repeat round 2.
- **Rejoin color B,** repeat round 3.

Repeat last 2 rounds eight more times. Bind off as follows: with main color A, K2tog *, P1, pass previous st over, K2tog, pass previous st over, repeat from * to end. Weave in ends. Block.

CHAPTER 5

Lace

An extraordinary range of lacy and textured effects can be achieved by manipulating yarn in various ingenious ways. The following pages explain how to create many of these effects and show how to apply them in a selection of scarves that will be treasured for years to come.

Lace step-by-step

Holes in lace knitting are formed by working a decorative increase—the type used depends on the size of the hole required and the stitch being worked. The entrelac technique looks like magic, with the changing direction of the stitches forming a patchwork fabric. The effect is achieved by turning rows, increasing and decreasing, and picking up stitches.

Decorative increases

A yarn-over (yo) is a strand of yarn looped over the right-hand needle between two stitches. The way it is worked differs depending on the position of the yarn at the start and where it needs to be to work the next stitch.

Yo between 2 knit stitches
Bring the yarn to the front between the needles. Knit the next stitch, taking the yarn across the needle and making one stitch.

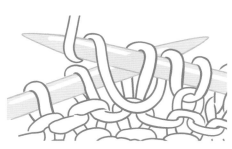

Yo between 2 purl stitches
Take the yarn over the needle from front to back, around the needle, and to the front. Purl the next stitch. Wrapping the yarn around the needle makes a stitch.

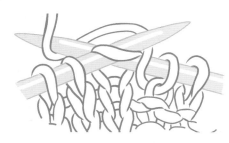

Yo between a purl and a knit stitch
Take the yarn over the needle from front to back and knit the next stitch. The yarn lays across the right-hand needle, so making a stitch.

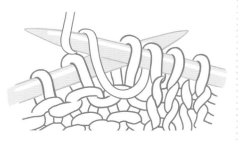

Yo between a knit and a purl stitch
Bring yarn to the front between the needles, then take it over and around the needle, and purl the next stitch. Wrapping the yarn makes the next stitch.

Entrelac

In this technique, each block has twice as many rows as stitches; this example is based on a block size of 10 stitches by 20 rows. Changing color for each row of blocks will help you understand the method.

1 Using the first color, cast on a multiple of 10 stitches (40 stitches shown here).
1st base triangle: P2, turn, K2, turn, P3, turn, K3, turn. Continue in this way, purling 1 more stitch from the left-hand needle on every alternate row until there are 10 stitches on the right-hand needle. Do not turn. Leave these 10 stitches on the needle.
2nd and following base triangles: Work as for 1st base triangle.

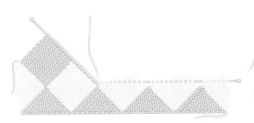

2 The first row of blocks begins (and ends) with a side triangle. Change to the second color.

1st side triangle: K2, turn, P2, turn, Ktw, ssk, turn, P3, turn, Ktw, K1, ssk, turn, P4, turn. Continue in this way until the row "Ktw, K7, ssk" has been worked. Do not turn. Leave these 10 stitches on the needle.

Block: Pick up and knit 10 stitches from the side edge of the base triangle (1 stitch from every alt row). Turn, p10, turn. * K9, ssk, turn, p10 *, repeat from * to * until all 10 stitches of the next base triangle have been decreased. Do not turn. Repeat this block in all the spaces between the base triangles.

2nd side triangle: Pick up and knit 10 stitches from the side edge of the last base triangle, turn, P2tog, P8, turn, K9, turn. P2tog, P7, turn, K8. Continue in this way until 1 stitch remains. Turn and slip this stitch onto the left-hand needle.

3 The second side of blocks has no side triangle.

Block: P1, pick up and purl 9 sts from the side ege of the previous side triangle, turn, K10, turn. *P9, P2tog, turn, K10*, repeat from * to * until all 10 stitches of the next block have been decreased. Do not turn.

2nd and following blocks: Begin by picking up and purling 10 stitches from the side edge of the next block, then work the new block in the same way.

4 The last row of triangles makes a straight edge at the top of the work. Change to the first color.

1st triangle P1, pick up and purl 9 sts from the side ege of the side triangle, turn, K10, turn. P2tog, P7, P2tog, turn, K8, turn. Continue in this way until turn, K2 has been worked. Turn, P1, P2tog, turn, K2, turn, P3tog. One stitch remains.

2nd triangle Pick up and purl 9 sts from the side edge of the next block and then complete the triangle in the same way as the first triangle. Repeat the 2nd triangle to the end of the row.

Lace Library

Lace stitch patterns are perfect for improving the drape of a project, injecting a feminine note, and for extending a limited amount of yarn. The warmth of a scarf need not be compromised because the air trapped in its folds provides warmth. All these lace patterns can be used as an all-over stitch pattern or as panels or edgings.

Slanted lace pattern

A light and delicate fabric on the bias—it doesn't get much better than that for a simple, single-stitch pattern scarf with pretty, feminine appeal.

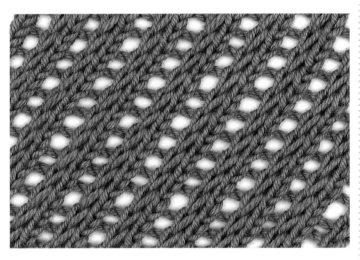

- **Row 1 (RS)** K1, wyib slip 1st, yo, K2tog; repeat from * to last st, K1.
- **Row 2** Purl.
These 2 rows form the pattern.

Customize your scarf:
Substitute Section 1 pattern used in Lace Ruffle Shawl (page 110).

Feather and fan

This classic lace pattern has excellent drape, producing a solid fabric with lacy areas. It is an excellent substitute both for lace stitch patterns and some more solid stitch patterns.

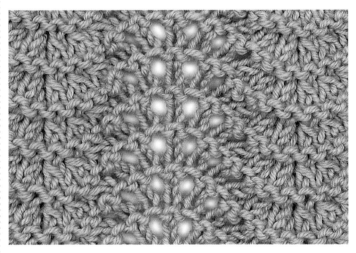

- **Row 1 (RS)** Knit.
- **Row 2** Purl.
- **Row 3** [K2tog] 3 times, [yo, K1] 5 times, yo, [ssk] 3 times.
- **Row 4** Knit.
These 4 rows form the stitch pattern.

Customize your scarf:
Substitute the Lace Pattern 2 edging on Lace Triangle Shawl (page 118).

Lace cable

This lace pattern does not actually include any cables—the effect is achieved by the judicious use of decreases and yarn-overs.

Front

Back

Note
Check your stitch count on rows 4–6 only.

- **Row 1 (RS)** *P3, K3, yo; repeat from * to last 3 sts, P3.
- **Row 2** *K3, P4; repeat from * to last 3 sts, K3.
- **Row 3** *P3, K1, K2tog, yo, K1; repeat from * to last 3 sts, P3.
- **Row 4** *K3, P2, P2tog; repeat from * to last 3 sts, K3.
- **Row 5** *P3, K1, yo, K2tog; repeat from * to last 3 sts, P3.
- **Row 6** *K3, P3; repeat from * to last 3 sts, K3.

These 6 rows form the stitch pattern.

Customize your scarf:
Substitute the Slim Cables pattern in Sugar and Spice (page 68).

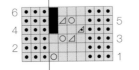

Lace chevron

This looks good along a scarf edge. Work the repeat so that the two decreases are in the center of the panel or work as two five-stitch panels, decreasing one stitch in from the edge.

- **Row 1 (RS)** *K1, yo, K2, slip 1st, K1, psso, K2tog, K2, yo, K1; repeat from * to end.
- **Row 2** Purl.
- **Row 3** *K2, yo, K1, slip 1st, K1, psso, K2tog, K1, yo, K2; repeat from * to end.
- **Row 4** Purl.
- **Row 5** *K3, yo, slip 1st, K1, psso, K2tog, yo, K3; repeat from * to end.
- **Row 6** Purl.

These 6 rows form the stitch pattern.

Customize your scarf:
Work along the outer edge of Lace Triangle Shawl (page 118).

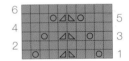

Ladder and gate

This pattern has been worked on a rib stitch pattern to create a reversible fabric. The lightweight fabric that it creates makes a useful edging but swatch carefully before using in a panel.

Cat's paw lace

These rosettes of yarn-overs are useful for weaving strands of yarn either vertically, horizontally, or in rounds, that are then secured in the fabric or are allowed to hang beyond the edge.

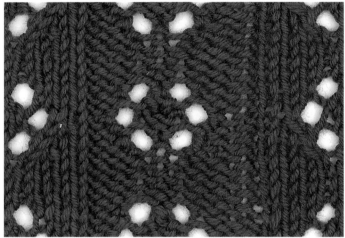

- **Row 1 (WS)** *K5, P5; repeat from * to end.
- **Row 2** *K1, slip 1st, K1, psso, K2, [yo] twice, *P2, P3tog, P2, [yo] twice, K2, K3tog, [yo] twice; repeat from * to last 5 sts, P2, P2togtbl, p1.
- **Row 3** *K4, purl then knit into the two yo, P5, purl then knit into the two yo, K5, purl then knit into the two yo; repeat from * to last 4 sts, P4.

These 3 rows form the stitch pattern.

Customize your scarf:
Work along the outer edges of Simple but Sublime (page 42).

- **Row 1 (RS)** *K9, P9; repeat from * to last 9 sts, K9.
- **Row 2** *P9, K9; repeat from * to last 9 sts, P9.
- **Rows 3–4** Repeat rows 1–2.
- **Row 5** *K2, K2tog, yo, K1, yo, slip 1st, K1, psso, K2, P2, P2togtbl, yo, P1, yo, P2tog, P2, repeat from * to last 9 sts, K2, K2tog, yo, K1, yo, slip 1st, K1, psso, K2.
- **Row 5** Repeat row 6.
- **Row 7** *K1, K2tog, yo, K3, yo, slip 1st, K1, psso, K1, P1, P2togtbl, yo, P3, yo, P2tog, P1; repeat from * to last 9 sts, K1, K2tog, yo, K3, yo, slip 1st, K1, psso, K1.
- **Row 8** Repeat row 6.
- **Row 9** *K3, yo, slip 1st, K2tog, psso, yo, K3, P3, yo, slip 1st, P2togtbl, P3; repeat from * to last 9 sts, K3, yo, slip 1st, K2tog, psso, yo, K3.
- **Row 10** Repeat row 6.

These 10 rows form the pattern.

Customize your scarf:
Work one nine-stitch motif block in the center of an entrelac square of Entrelac Shawl (page 114).

△ *p3tog*

⊘ *double yarn over*

◣/ *purl, then knit into double yarn over*

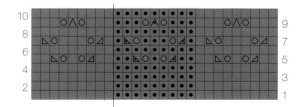

Zigzag lace

For a garter stitch pattern, this motif has excellent drape and visual appeal. It is a perfect all-over pattern for a design-as-you-go scarf. The garter stitch will enhance most yarns and the eyelets promise endless embellishment potential.

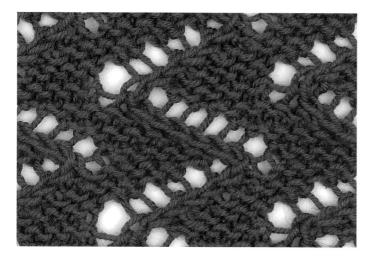

- **Row 1 (RS)** K7, k2tog, yo, *K6, K2tog, yo; repeat from * to last st, K1.
- **Row 2** K2, yo, P2tog, *K6, yo, P2tog; repeat from * to last 6 sts, K6.
- **Row 3** K5, K2tog, yo, *K6, K2tog, yo; repeat from * to last 3 sts, K3.
- **Row 4** K4, yo, P2tog, *K6, yo, P2tog; repeat from * to last 4 sts, K4.
- **Row 5** K3, K2tog, yo, *K6, K2tog, yo; repeat from * to last 5 sts, K5.
- **Row 6** K6, yo, P2tog, *K6, yo, P2tog; repeat from * to last 2 sts, K5.
- **Row 7** K1, K2tog, yo, *K6, K2tog, yo; repeat from * to last 7 sts, K7.
- **Row 8** K7, P2togtbl, yo, *K6, P2togtbl, yo; repeat from * to last st, K1.
- **Row 9** K2, yo, slip 1st, K1, psso, *K6, yo slip 1st, K1, psso; repeat from * to last 6 sts, K6.
- **Row 10** K5, P2togtbl, yo, *K6, P2togtbl, yo; repeat from * to last 3 sts, K3.
- **Row 11** K4, yo, slip 1st, K1, psso, *K6, yo, slip 1st, K1, psso; repeat from * to last 4 sts, K4.
- **Row 12** K3, P2togtbl, yo, *K6, P2togtbl, yo; repeat from * to last 5 sts, K5.
- **Row 13** K6, yo, slip 1st, K1, psso, *K6, yo slip 1st, K1, psso; repeat from * to last 2 sts, K5.
- **Row 14** K1, P2togtbl, yo, *K6, P2togtbl, yo; repeat from * to last 7 sts, K7.

These 14 rows form the stitch pattern.

Customize your scarf:

Cast on 26 stitches and substitute this pattern for that of Climbing Vines Shawl (page 122).

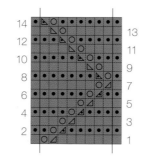

Fern lace

This simple fern lace pattern looks good with the addition of small bobbles or beads. The beads will add weight to the fabric and improve the drape.

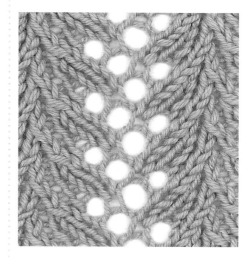

- **Row 1 (WS)** Purl.
- **Row 2** K3, *yo, K2, slip 1st, K1, psso, K2tog, K2, yo, K1; repeat from * to last st, K1.
- **Row 3** Purl.
- **Row 4** K2, *yo, K2, slip 1st, K1, psso, K2tog, K2, yo, K1; repeat from * to last 2 sts, K2.

These 4 rows form the stitch pattern.

Customize your scarf:

Cast on 13 sts and work as for Cables and Baubles (page 64), replacing the existing stitch pattern.

Lace Ruffle Shawl

Holey knitting! No really, I made holes in my knitting on purpose. That is the essence of lace knitting. It's all about arithmetic with plusses (increases) and minuses (decreases) that add up to a fashionable accessory. Get the math right and I promise the final sum will be beautiful.

Yarn

- Medium-weight yarn (#4), 100% baby alpaca, 100 yd (110 m), 3½ oz (50 g); 4 balls main color: indigo; 1 ball contrast color: white

Needles & notions

- US 8 (5 mm) circular needles in two lengths: 24 in (60 cm) and 40 in (102 cm) or longer
- Tapestry needle
- 20 stitch markers

Gauge

20 stitches equal 4 in (10 cm) in garter stitch

Size

Shawl measures 54 in (137 cm) long, 8 in (20 cm) wide

Special abbreviations

- **pm:** Place marker
- **sm:** Slip marker
- **sK2togpo:** Slip 1 knitwise, knit 2 together, pass slip st over

Section 1

With the shorter needles, cast on 20 sts.
- **Row 1** K1, Kfb, K to last 3 sts, K2tog, K1.
- **Row 2** K.
- Repeat these 2 rows until scarf measures 40 in (102 cm) ending row 2. Do not bind off.

Section 2

Change to longer needle. Work section 1, row 1 again. Pick up and knit 175 sts along the edge of section 1 (195 sts).
- **Row 1** P.
- **Row 2 (RS)** K1, P1, K1, yo, * pm, K18, pm, yo, K1, yo, repeat from * to last 21 sts, pm, K18, pm, yo, K1, P1, K1 (215 sts).
- **Row 3 and all WS rows** P1, K1, P to last 2 sts slipping all markers, K1, P1.
- **Row 4** K1, P1, K2, yo, * sm, K18, sm, yo, K3, yo, repeat from * to 18 sts before last marker, sm, K18, sm, yo, K2, P1, K1 (235 sts).
- **Row 6** K1, P1, K3, yo, * sm, K18, sm, yo, K5, yo, repeat from * to 18 sts before last marker, sm, K18, sm, yo, K3, P1, K1 (255 sts).
- **Row 8** K1, P1, K4, yo, *sm, K18, sm, [yo, K1] twice, yo, sK2togpo, yo, [K1, yo] twice, repeat from * to 18 sts before last marker, sm, K18, sm, yo, K4, P1, K1 (293 sts).

■ **Row 10** K1, P1, K5, yo, * sm, [P2tog] 3 times, yo, [P1, yo] 6 times, [P2tog] 3 times, sm, yo, [K3, yo, K1, yo] twice, K3, yo, repeat from * to 18 sts before last marker, sm, [P2tog] 3 times, yo, [P1, yo] 6 times, [P2tog] 3 times, sm, yo, K5, P1, K1 (359 sts).

■ **Row 12** K1, P1, K6, yo, * sm, K19, sm, yo, [K5, yo, K1, yo] twice, K5, yo, repeat from * to 19 sts before last marker, P19, yo, knit to last 2 sts, P1, K1 (415 sts).

■ **Row 14** K1, P1, K7, yo, * sm, K19, sm, yo, K3, yo, sK2togpo, yo, K3, yo, ssk, K1, K2tog, yo, K3, yo, sK2togpo, yo, K3, yo, repeat from * to 19 sts before last marker, K19, sm, yo, K7, P1, K1 (435 sts).

■ **Row 16** K1, P1, K8, yo, * sm, K19, sm, yo, K5, yo, K1, yo, K5, yo, sK2togpo, yo, K5, yo, K1, yo, K5, yo, repeat from * to 19 sts before last marker, K19, sm, yo, K8, P1, K1 (491 sts).

■ **Row 18** K1, P1, K9, yo, * sm, [P2tog] 3 times, yo [P1, yo] 7 times, [P2tog] 3 times, sm, [yo, K7, yo, K1] 3 times, yo, K7, yo, repeat from * to 19 sts before last marker, [P2tog] 3 times, yo, [P1, yo] 7 times, [P2tog] 3 times, sm, yo, K9, P1, K1 (583 sts).

■ **Row 20** K1, P1, K10, yo, * sm, K21, sm, yo, K1, yo, [ssk, K3, K2tog, yo, K3, yo] 3 times, ssk, K3, K2tog, yo, K1, yo, repeat from * to 21 sts before last marker, K21, sm, yo, K10, P1, K1 (603 sts).

■ **Row 22** K1, P1, K11, yo, * sm, K21, sm, [yo, K1] 3 times, yo, [ssk, K1, K2tog, yo, K5, yo] 3 times, ssk, K1, K2tog, [yo, K1] 3 times, yo, repeat from * to 21 sts before last marker, K21, sm, yo, K11, P1, K1 (675 sts).

■ **Row 24** K1, P1, K12, yo, *sm, K21, sm, [yo, K1] twice, yo, K3, [yo, K1] twice, [yo, sK2togpo, yo, ssk, K3, K2tog] 3 times, yo, sK2togpo, [yo, K1] twice, yo, K3, [yo, K1] twice, yo, repeat from * to 21 sts before last marker, K21, sm, yo, K12, P1, K1 (711 sts).

■ **Row 26** K1, P1, K13, yo, * sm, [P2tog] 3 times, yo, [P1, yo] 9 times, [P2tog] 3 times, sm, [yo, K1] twice, yo, K3, yo, sK2togpo, yo, K3, yo, K1, [yo, sK2togpo, yo, ssk, K1, K2tog] 3 times, yo, sK2togpo, yo, K1, yo, K3, yo, sK2togpo, yo, K3, [yo, K1] twice, yo, repeat from * to 21 sts before last marker, P2tog 3 times, yo, [P1, yo] 9 times, P2tog 3 times, sm, yo, K13, P1, K1 (767 sts).

■ **Row 28** K1, P1, K14, yo, * sm, K25, sm, yo, K2tog, [yo, K3, yo, sK2togpo] twice, yo, ssk, [yo, K3, yo, sK2togpo] 3 times, yo, K3, yo, K2tog, yo, [sK2togpo, yo, K3, yo] twice, ssk, yo, repeat from * to 25 sts before last marker, K25, sm, yo, K14, P1, K1 (787 sts).

■ Change to color B, K 2 rows.

■ Change to main color, K 2 rows.

■ Repeat last 4 rows once more.

Finishing

Bind off loosely. Weave in ends and block.

Notes

Section 1 may be worked on straight needles. The lace ruffle is worked on long circular needles to better accommodate the many stitches.

GARTER STITCH EDGE
The last eight rows are worked in knit stitch and stop the edge curling but this can be replaced by any stitch pattern with a similar quality.

Entrelac Shawl

Entrelac often looks as if it is woven. In this shawl, I wanted to weave together various lace-knitting patterns. The center section is open and airy while the edges are more intricate with mitered corners, resulting in a one-of-a-kind shawl for the more experienced knitter that is both classic and fashion-forward.

Yarn

Bulky yarn (#3), 60% baby suri, 40% fine merino, 162 yd (100 m), 3½ oz (100 g); 4 balls

Needles & notions

- US 9 (5.5 mm) circular knitting needle, length at least 40 in (100 cm)
- Tapesty needle
- 8 stitch markers

Gauge

16 sts equal 4 in (10 cm) in stockinette stitch.

Size

Shawl measures 40 in (101 cm) long, 15 in (38 cm) wide

Special abbreviations

- **ppso:** Pass previous st over
- **sK2togpo:** Sl1 knitwise, K2 together, pass slip st over

Making the shawl

Entrelac panel
Cast on 60 sts.

Base triangles
- **Row 1** K2, turn.
- **Row 2** P2.
- **Row 3** K3, turn.
- **Row 4** P3.
- **Row 5** K4, turn.
- **Row 6** P4.
- **Row 7** K5, turn.
- **Row 8** P5.
- **Row 9** K6, turn.
- **Row 10** P6.
- **Row 11** K7, turn.
- **Row 12** P7.
- **Row 13** K8, turn.
- **Row 14** P8.
- **Row 15** K9, turn.
- **Row 16** P9.

- **Row 17** K10, place marker, do not turn. Repeat from rows 1–17, ending all P rows at marker 5 more times, ending with K10, turn.

Tier 1: Left-side triangle
- **Row 1 (WS)** P2, turn.
- **Row 2** Kfb, K1.
- **Row 3** Wyif, sl1 purlwise, P1, P2tog, turn.
- **Row 4** K1, Kfb, K1.
- **Row 5** Wyif, sl1 purlwise, P2, P2tog, turn.
- **Row 6 and all RS rows** Knit to last 2 sts, Kfb, K1.
- **Row 7** Wyif, sl1 purlwise, P3, P2tog, turn.
- **Row 9** Wyif, sl1 purlwise, P4, P2tog.
- **Row 11** Wyif, sl1 purlwise, P5, P2tog.
- **Row 13** Wyif, sl1 purlwise, P6, P2tog.
- **Row 15** Wyif, sl1 purlwise, P7, P2tog.
- **Row 17** Wyif, sl1 purlwise, P8, P2tog (10 sts), slip marker, continue to Tier 1 without turning.

Base triangles

Tier 1

Tier 2

First square

- **Row 1 Set up row (WS)** With wrong side facing, pick up and P 10 sts along selvage edge of next square, turn.
- **Row 2 RS rows** K2, *(yo, K2tog), repeat from * 3 more times ending at marker, turn.
- **Row 3** Wyif, sl1 purlwise, P8, P2tog, turn.

Repeat last two rows 9 more times, ending at marker. **Do not turn on last row.** Slip marker. Repeat last 21 rows 4 more times to end of row, do not turn (5 squares, 60 sts in all).

Right-side triangle

- **Row 1 Set up row (WS)** Place marker. Pick up and P 10 sts along selvage of next square, turn.
- **Row 2 and all RS rows** Knit to marker, turn (10 sts).
- **Row 3** Wyif, sl1 purlwise, P to last two stitches, P2tog, turn (9 sts).

Repeat last 2 rows until 2 sts remain.

- **Next row** K2.
- **Following row** P2tog, turn.

Tier 2: First square

- **Row 1 Set up row RS** Wyib, sl1 purlwise, remove marker, pick up and knit 9 sts along selvage of next square, K1, ppso (10 sts).
- **Row 2** P2tog, P8 (9 sts).
- **Row 3** Wyib, sl1 purlwise, K1,* [yo, ssk] repeat 4 more times, turn (10 sts).

Repeat the last 2 rows 9 more times, ending at marker. **Do not turn.** Slip marker.

Second square

- **Row 1 Set up row (RS)** Pick up and knit 10 sts along selvage of next square, K1, ppso (10 sts).

Repeat rows 2 and 3 on First Square, 9 times in all, ending at marker. Do not turn. Slip marker. Repeat Second Square 4 more times to end of row (6 squares, 60 sts in all).

Work Left-side Triangle, Tier 1, Right-side Triangle, Tier 2, Left-side Triangle, Tier 1, and Right-side Triangle.

Final tier triangles

Wyib, sl1 purlwise, remove marker.

- **Row 1 RS** With RS facing, pick up and knit 9 sts

along selvage of next square or triangle, K1, ppso (10 sts).

- **Row 2 and all WS rows** P to end, turn.
- **Row 3** K2tog, K7, ssk, turn (9 sts).
- **Row 5** K2tog, K6, ssk, turn (8 sts).
- **Row 7** K2tog, K5, ssk, turn (7 sts).
- **Row 9** K2tog, K4, ssk, turn (6 sts).
- **Row 11** K2tog, K3, ssk, turn (5 sts).
- **Row 13** K2tog, K2, ssk, turn (4 sts).
- **Row 15** K2tog, K1, ssk, turn (3 sts).
- **Row 17** K2tog, ssk, turn (2 sts).
- **Row 19** Sl 2 knitwise, K1, pass both sl sts over, ending at marker (1 st). Remove marker.

Repeat rows 1–19, 5 more times across row. Fasten off.

Lace panels

With RS facing, pick up and knit 36 sts from one side edge of entrelac panel.

- **Row 1 WS** P to end.
- **Row 2 RS** K3, [yo, ssk] 15 times, K3.
- **Row 3 and 4** P to end.
- **Row 5** K to end.
- **Row 6** P1, * P2, yo, ssk, K1, K2tog, yo, P2 *, K9, yo, K1, yo, K3, sK2togpo, repeat from * to * once more, P1.
- **Row 7 and all WS rows** K3, P5, K2, P16, K2, P5, K3.
- **Row 8** P1, * P2, K1, yo, sK2togpo, yo, K1, P2 *, K10, yo, K1, yo, K2, sK2togpo, repeat from * to * once more, P1.
- **Row 10** P1, * P2, yo, ssk, K1, K2tog, yo, P2 *, K3tog, K4, yo, K1, yo, K3, yo, K1, yo, K1, sK2togpo, repeat from * to * once more, P1.
- **Row 12** P1, * P2, K1, yo, sK2togpo, yo, K1, P2 *, K3tog, K3, yo, K1, yo, K9, repeat from * to * once more, P1.
- **Row 14** P1, * P2, yo, ssk, K1, K2tog, yo, P2 *, K3tog, K2, yo, K1, yo, K10, repeat from * to * once more, P1.
- **Row 16** P1, * P2, K1, yo, sK2togpo, yo, K1, P2 *, K3tog, K1, yo, K1, yo, K3, yo, K1, yo, K4, sK2togpo, repeat from * to * once more, P1.

(Row 17 As row 7.)

- **Row 18–21** Work rows 6–9 once more.
- **Row 22** P1, * P2, yo, ssk, K1, K2tog, yo, P2 *, K11, yo, Kl, yo, K1, sK2togpo, repeat from * to * once more, P1.

(Row 23 As row 7.)

- **Row 24** P3, K1, yo, sK2togpo, yo, K1, P20, K1, yo, sK2togpo, yo, K1, P3.
- **Row 25** K3, P5, K20, P5, K3.

Leave these sts on a holder.
Repeat these 25 rows on the opposite side edge.

Outer border

Using long-length circular needle, * K36 from holder at one side edge, place marker, pick up and K 1 st at corner, place marker, pick up and K 24 sts from side edge of lace panel, 60 sts from long edge of entrelac panel, 24 sts from side edge of next lace panel (total of 108 sts from one long edge), place marker, pick up and K 1 st at corner, place marker, repeat from * once more (292 sts).

- **Round 1** * [K2tog] 3 times, [yo, K1] 6 times, [K2tog] 3 times *, repeat from * to * once more to marker, yo, sm, K1, sm, yo, repeat from * to * 6 times to marker, yo, sm, K1, sm, yo, repeat from * to * twice to marker, yo, sm, K1, sm, yo, repeat from * to * 6 times to marker, yo, sm, K1, sm, yo (300 sts).
- **Round 2** * K to m, yo, sm, K1, sm, yo, repeat from * 3 more times (308 sts).
- **Round 3** * P to m, yo, sm, K1, sm, yo, repeat from * 3 more times (316 sts).
- **Rounds 4 and 5** Repeat rounds 2 and 3 (332 sts).
- **Round 6** K5, * [K2tog] 3 times, [yo, K1] 6 times, [K2tog] 3 times *, repeat from * to * once more, K5 to marker, yo, sm, K1, sm, yo, K5, repeat from * to * 6 times, K5 to marker, yo, sm, K1, sm, yo, K5, repeat from * to * twice, K5 to marker, yo, sm, K1, sm, yo, K5, repeat from * to * 6 times, K5 to marker, yo, sm, K1, sm, yo (340 sts).
- **Rounds 7–10** As rounds 2–5 (372 sts).

Finishing

Knit 4 rows and bind off loosely as follows:
*P2tog, sl this st back to left-hand needle, repeat from * to end. Weave in ends and block.

Lace Triangle Shawl

Lace knitting is the apex of the knitter's craft. It will test your skills, resolve, and attention to detail. I chose to knit this lacy shawl in a sportweight yarn to create a dramatic drape. The quilt pattern is introduced in the first section of the shawl, followed by a lace diamond motif, and finally a generous lace edge.

Making the shawl

Begin at center of longest side.
Set up rows.
Cast on 3 sts.
Knit 6 rows.
- **Next row** K3, pick up and K 3 sts from left side, pick up and K 3 sts from cast-on edge (9 sts).
- **Following row** K3, P3, K3.

Quilted pattern

All sl sts are slipped purlwise.
- **WS rows** K3, P to last 3 sts, K3.
- **Row 1** K3, yo, K1, yo, place marker, K1, yo, K1, yo, K3 (13 sts).
- **Row 2 and all WS rows** K3, P (skipping marker) to last 3 sts, K3.
- **Row 3** K3, yo, K3, yo, sm, K1, yo, K3, yo, K3 (17 sts).
- **Row 5** K3, yo, knit to marker, yo, sm, K1, yo, knit to last 3 sts, yo, K3 (21 sts).
- **Row 7** K3, yo, K1, wyif sl5, K1, yo, sm, K1, yo, K1, wyif, sl5, K1, yo, K3 (25 sts).
- **Row 9** As row 5 (29 sts).
- **Row 11** K3 , yo, K5, lkpo, K5 to marker, yo, sm, K1, yo, K5, lkpo, K5 to last 3 sts, yo, K3 (33 sts).

- **Row 13** K3, yo, * K1, wyif sl5, * repeat * to * to 1 st before marker, K1, yo, sm, K1, yo, repeat * to * to last 4 sts, K1, yo, K3 (37 sts).
- **Row 15** As row 5 (41 sts).
- **Row 17** K3, yo, * K5, lkpo, * repeat * to * to 5 sts before marker, K5, yo, sm, K1, yo, repeat * to * to last 8 sts, K5, yo, K3 (45 sts).
- **(Row 18** As row 2.)
Repeat rows 13–18, 16 more times (141 sts).

Lace pattern 1

- **Row 1** K3, yo, * K1, yo, ssk, K1, K2tog, yo, * repeat * to * to 1 st before marker, K1, yo, sm, K1, yo, repeat * to * to last 4 sts, K1, yo, K3 (145 sts).
- **Row 2 and all WS rows** K3, P to last 3 sts, K3.
- **Row 3** K3, yo, * K3, yo, sK2togpo, yo, * repeat * to * to 3 sts before marker, K3, yo, sm, K1, yo, repeat * to * to last 6 sts, K3, yo, K3 (149 sts).
- **Row 5** K3, yo, K2, * K1, K2tog, yo, K1, yo, ssk, * repeat * to * to 3 sts before marker, K3, yo, sm, K1, yo, K2, repeat * to *to last 6 sts, K3, yo, K3 (153 sts).
- **Row 7** K3, yo, K2, * yo, sk2togpo, yo,

Yarn

Sportweight yarn (#2), alpaca, 110 yd (100 m), 1¾ oz (50 g), 4 balls

Needles & notions

- US 8 (5 mm) knitting needles
- Tapestry needle
- 1 stitch marker
- Blocking pins

Gauge

20 sts equal 4 in (10 cm) in stockinette stitch

Size

Shawl measures 44 in (113 cm) wide, 20 in (51 cm) high

Special abbreviations

- **lkpo:** Lift strand 4 rows below onto right-hand needle, K next st, pass strand over and off needle.
- **sm:** Slip marker
- **sk2togpo:** Slip 1 knitwise, knit 2 together, pass slip st over.

BACK VIEW

This pretty shawl looks just as good viewed from the back, where the detailing of the stitch patterns can fully be seen.

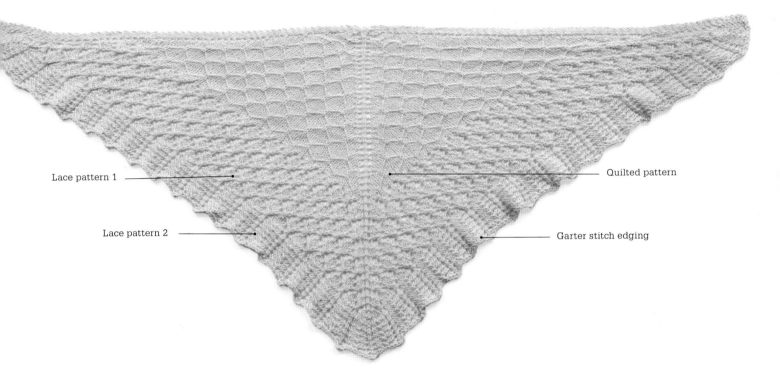

Lace pattern 1

Quilted pattern

Lace pattern 2

Garter stitch edging

K3, * repeat * to * to 5 sts before marker, yo, sk2togpo, yo, K2, yo, sm, K1, yo, K2, repeat * to * to last 8 sts, yo, sk2togpo, yo, K2, yo, K3. (157 sts).

- **Row 9** K3, yo, K2, * K2tog, yo, K1, yo, ssk, K1, * repeat * to * to 2 sts before marker, K2, yo, sm, K1, yo, K2, * repeat * to * to last 4 sts, K1, yo, K3. (161 sts).

- **Row 11** K3, yo, K1, * yo, sk2togpo, yo, K3, * * repeat * to * to 4 sts before marker, yo, sk2togpo, yo, K1, yo, sm, K1, yo, K1, * repeat * to * to last 7 sts, yo, sk2togpo, yo, K1, yo, K3. (165 sts).

- **Row 13** K3, yo, * K1, K2tog, yo, K1, yo, ssk, * * repeat * to * to 1 st before marker, K1, yo, sm, K1, yo, * repeat * to * to last 4 sts, K1, yo, K3. (169 sts).

- **Row 15** K3, yo, K1, K2tog, yo, * K3, yo, sk2togpo, yo, * * repeat * to * to 6 sts before marker, K3, yo, ssk, K1, yo, sm, K1, yo, K1, K2tog, yo, * repeat * to

* to last 9 sts, K3, yo, ssk, K1, yo, K3. (173 sts).

- **Row 17** K3, yo, * K2tog, yo, K1, yo, ssk, K1, * * repeat * to * to 5 sts before marker, K2tog, yo, K1, yo, ssk, yo, sm, K1, yo, * repeat * to * to last 8 sts, K2tog, yo, K1, yo, ssk, yo, K3 (177 sts).

- **Row 19** K3, yo, K2tog, yo, * K3, yo, sk2togpo, yo, * repeat * to * to 5 sts before marker, K3, yo, ssk, yo, sm, K1, yo, K2tog, yo, * repeat * to * to last 8 sts, K3, yo, ssk, yo, K3 (181 sts).

- **Row 21** K3, yo, K2, * yo, ssk, K1, K2tog, yo, K1, * * repeat * to * to 1 st before marker, K1, yo, sm, K1, yo, K2, * repeat * to * to last 4 sts, K1, yo, K3 (185 sts).

- **Row 23** K3, yo, K4, * yo, sk2togpo, yo, K3, * * repeat * to * to 1 st before marker, K1, yo, sm, K1, yo, K4, repeat * to * to last 4 sts, K1, yo, K3 (189 sts).

- **Row 24** As row 2.
Repeat rows 1–4 once again, removing marker on last row (197 sts).

Lace pattern 2

- **Row 1** K3, * yo, K5, yo, K1* * repeat * to * to last 2 sts, K2 (261 sts).
- **Row 2 and all WS rows** K3, P to last 3 sts, K3.
- **Row 3** K3, * yo, K2, sk2togpo, K2, yo, K1, * * repeat * to * to last 2 sts, K2.
- **(Row 4** As row 2.)

Repeat rows 3 and 4, 5 more times, and row 3 once again.

Finishing

Knit 4 rows and bind off loosely as follows: P2tog, *slip stitch back onto left-hand needle, P2tog, repeat from * to end. Weave in all ends. Block lace to define stitches, using blocking pins to define points on cast-off edge.

Climbing Vines Shawl

My design process starts with the stitch pattern. Next, I turn to how it will look using different yarns. For example, how will it drape in a sportweight alpaca versus a bulky wool? So I swatch. The Climbing Vines stitch pattern has movement and texture and I like it because it works well in a wide range of yarns.

Making the scarf

Cast on 27 sts.

- **Row 1 (RS)** K1, *K2tog, K1, yo, K1, slip 1, K1, psso, K2; repeat from * to last 2 sts, K2 (24 sts).
- **Row 2 and all WS rows** P to end.
- **Row 3** *K2tog, K1, [yo, K1] twice, slip 1, K1, psso; repeat from * to last 3 sts, K3.
- **Row 5** K2, *yo, K3, yo, K1, slip 1, K1, psso, K1; repeat from * to last st, K1 (27 sts).
- **Row 7** K4, *K2tog, K1, yo, K1, slip 1, K1, psso, K2 repeat from * to last 7 sts, K2tog, K1, yo, K1, slip 1, K1, psso, K1 (24 sts).
- **Row 9** K3, *K2tog, K1, [yo, K1] twice, slip 1, K1, psso, repeat from * to end of row.
- **Row 11** K2, *K2tog, K1, yo, K3, yo, K1 repeat from * to last stitch, K1 (27 sts).
- **Row 12** P to end.

Repeat rows 1–12 until shawl measures 50 in (127 cm) or length required, ending row 6 or 12.

Bind off. Weave in ends and block.

Making the fringes

Cut 24 in (61 cm) strands of yarn and use the crochet hook to make a fringe at each end, as shown in this photograph (4 strands per knot).

Yarn

Super bulky-weight yarn (#6), 50% merino, 50% alpaca wool: 45 yd (41 m)/3½ oz (100 g): 5 hanks

✕ Needles & notions

- US 17 (13 mm) knitting needles or size needed to obtain gauge
- Large crochet hook
- Tapestry needle

Gauge

8 sts and 8 rows in stitch pattern equals 4 in (10 cm) in bulky yarn

Size

Shawl measures 50 in (127 cm) long, 12 in (30 cm) wide excluding fringe

CHAPTER 6

Customizing Scarves

Some knitters like to make things; some knitters like to experiment with new techniques. Scarves make the perfect project for both kinds of knitter, especially when the exciting possibilities for customization are explored.

Developing your own designs

There is no mystery to designing—it involves taking elements you like and putting them together— but there are always some favorite combinations. They may be ideas you have seen in the stores, in catwalk photographs, or in your favorite knitting book or magazine. You will find that you will use some of these ideas again and again just because they work and are fun.

Edgings

Edgings that are worked across an edge can be knitted from stitches picked up along an edge or from cast on stitches. For edgings worked from the bottom (free) edge up to the top (fixed) edge, the top edge is sewn to the edge of the project after knitting.

Knitted edgings worked across an edge

Edgings that are worked across an edge can be knitted from stitches picked up along an edge or from cast on stitches. For edgings worked from the bottom (free) edge up to the top (fixed) edge, the top edge is sewn to the edge of the project after knitting. To work out how many stitches to pick up or cast on, work a swatch and calculate the number of stitches required for the scarf edge. It is often useful to double-check your

calculation by working a sample edging for the project gauge swatch. There are stitch directories full of decorative edgings and stores full of luxurious yarns—the choice is yours. Here are a few ideas to consider.

Flat lace edging

This simple edging is particularly useful because its row repeat means that it can be knitted until the desired length is reached. It could be worked in a contrasting yarn or in the same yarn as the project. An edging need not be a bold statement; a subtle contrast often works equally well. The few rows before the chevron are the Lace motif 1 pattern from the Lace Triangle Shawl on page 118. The pattern below is the Lace Pattern 2 from the same scarf with the triangle shaping removed.

Keep it neat
The trick to a neat line of picked-up and knitted stitches is to be consistent— to pick up and knit stitches in the same stitches or rows of the pattern repeat.

Multiple 12 stitches plus 3 stitches

With right side facing, evenly pick up and knit the required number of stitches along the edge.

Turn the work, K3, purl to the last two stitches, K3. This brings the yarn back to the right-hand edge ready to work a right-side row as indicated by the pattern.

- **Row 1** (RS) K3, *K4, yo, K1, yo, K4, slip 1, K2tog, psso; repeat from * to last 11 stitches, K4, yo, K1, yo, K7.
- **Row 2** K3, P2tog, purl until the last 5 stitches, P2tog, K3

Repeat the last two rows until the desired length is reached. Bind off.

FLAT LACE EDGING
The eyelets and panels of knitting make this edging perfect for embellishment and to hang tassels or pom-poms from.

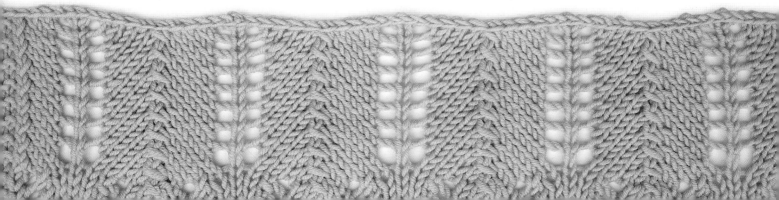

Lace frill

A lace frill edging produces volume with less weight. This frill uses a favorite design—take a lace pattern, work the yarn-overs but do not work all or any of the decreases. This does require some understanding of the pattern in order to keep the relationship between the yarn-overs correct but it is great fun and always produces some stitch ideas for the next project. This edging is based on a feather and fan pattern.

Multiple 17 stitches plus 4 stitches

With right side facing, evenly pick up and knit the required number of stitches along the edge.

- **Row 1** Knit.
- **Row 2** (RS) Knit.
- **Row 3** K2, purl to the last 2 stitches, K2.
- **Row 4** K2 * [K2tog] 3 times, [yo, K1] 5 times, yo, [ssk] 3 times; repeat from * to the last 2 sts, K2.
- **Row 5** Knit.

Rows 6–9 Starting with a knit row, work 4 rows in stockinette stitch.

- **Row 10** K2 * K3, [yo, K1] 11 times, yo, K2; repeat from * to the last 2 sts, K2.
- **Rows 11–15** Repeats 5th–9th rows.
- **Row 16** K2 * K3, [yo, K1] 23 times, yo, K2; repeat from * to the last 2 sts, K2.

Starting with a purl row, work 7 rows in stockinette stitch. Bind off.

Drop stitch edging

One approach to a knitted edging is to echo an element used in the project and perhaps add a visual twist to it. This edging pattern has been adapted from the dropped stitch pattern on page 48. Here, the stitch is not dropped on row 8, but on the bind-off row.

Multiple 8 stitches

With right side facing, evenly pick up and knit the required number of stitches along the edge.

Turn the work, K2, purl to the last two stitches, K2. This brings the yarn back to the right edge ready to work a right-side row as indicated by the pattern.

- **Row 1** (RS) K2, *K2, yo, K2, P4; repeat from * to last 6 stitches, K2, yo, K2, K2.
  - **Row 2** *K2, *P5, K4; repeat from * to last 7 stitches, P5, K2.
  - **Row 3** *K2, *K5, P4; repeat from * to last 7 stitches, K5, K2.
  - **Rows 4–7** Repeat rows 2 and 3, twice more.
- **Row 8** *K2, *p5, K2, yo, K2; repeat from * to last 7 stitches, P5, K2.
- **Row 9** *K2, *K5, P5; repeat from * to last 7 stitches, K5, K2.
- **Row 10** *K2, *P5, K5; repeat from * to last 7 stitches, P5, K2.

 BOX PLEATS

BOX PLEATS

Pleats and frills have a functional as well as decorative purpose, providing a snug fit around the neck.

picked up and knitted at regular intervals along the project edge and then worked into a decrease on a following row. If rows of the edging match or nearly match rows or stitches on the project, then plan the picked-up stitches accordingly.

Short-row frill

This is a good standard basic frill edging. The short-rows create the extra fabric required and the reverse stockinette stitch adds volume. One or both of these sections could be worked in other stitch patterns. This edging looks similar on both sides and could be knitted to an edge by picking up and knitting a stitch along an edge, then working a decrease on one of the following two rows.

Cast on 20 stitches.
- **Row 1** Purl.
- **Row 2** K16, w&t.
- **Row 3** Purl.
- **Row 4** K12, w&t.
- **Row 5** Purl.
- **Row 6** K8, w&t.
- **Row 7** Purl.
- **Row 8** K4, w&t.
- **Row 9** Purl.
- **Row 10** K4, [pick up the wrap loop and work together with the next stitch, K3] 4 times.

- **Rows 11–14** Repeat rows 9 and 10, twice more.
- **Bind-off row** [K1, pso] 4 times, drop the next stitch off the needle, [yo right needle, pso] 4 times; repeat from * to last 4 stitches, [K1, pso] 4 times.

Box pleats

This edging is especially neat and tidy and looks great adorned with buttons and embroidery.

Multiple 9 stitches plus 8 stitches

With right side facing evenly pick up and knit the required number of stitches along the edge.
- **Row 1** Purl.
- **Row 2** (RS) *slip 1 st purlwise, K6, slip 1 st purlwise, M1, K1, M1; repeat from * to last 8 stitches, slip 1 st purlwise, K6, slip 1 st purlwise.
- **Row 3 and each odd-numbered row** Purl.
- **Row 4** *Slip 1 st purlwise, K6, slip 1 st purlwise, [K1, M1] twice, K1; repeat from * to last 8 stitches, slip 1 st purlwise, K6, slip 1 st purlwise.
- **Row 6** *Slip 1 st purlwise, K6, slip 1 st purlwise, K1, wyif, slip 1 st purlwise, wyib, M1, K1, M1, wyif, slip 1 st purlwise, wyib, K1; repeat from * to last 8 stitches, slip 1 st purlwise, K6, slip 1 st purlwise.

- **Row 8** *slip 1 st purlwise, K6, slip 1 st purlwise, K1, wyif, slip 2 sts purlwise, wyib, M1, K1, M1, wyif slip 2 sts purlwise, wyib K1; repeat from * to last 8 stitches, slip 1 st purlwise, K6, slip 1 st purlwise.
- **Row 10** *slip 1 st purlwise, K6, slip 1 st purlwise, K1, wyif slip 3 sts purlwise, wyib M1, K1, M1, wyif slip 3 sts purlwise, wyib, K1; repeat from * to last 8 stitches, slip 1 st purlwise, K6, slip 1 st purlwise.
- **Bind-off row** *K1, [pso, K1] 8 times, pso, P4tog, pso, K1, pso, P4tog, pso, K1, pso; repeat from * to last 8 stitches. Bind off remaining stitches.

Knitted edgings worked along an edge

Edgings of this kind can be knitted to an edge at the end of a row or can be worked separately and sewn to an edge later. Start with a swatch of the edging you have chosen. Then, pin it and sew it to the project gauge swatch. There are two things to note. Does the inflexibility of the sewn seam restrict the edging and do rows of the edging match or nearly match the stitches or rows of the project swatch at regular intervals? If a sewn seam restricts an edging, consider knitting the edging to the project as it is worked. To do this, edge stitches are

BOBBLE EDGE

Most cable patterns worked along an edge will curl slightly and create an interesting edging.

- **Rows 11-16** Starting with a knit row, work in stockinette stitch.
- **Row 17** K4, purl to the end of the row. Repeat rows 2–17 until the desired length is reached. Bind off.

Bobble wrap edging

The Bobble Wrap on page 76 inspired this edging. The textured strip gives this a very flexible edge that can be gathered or stretched slightly as it is sewn to the project edge. The bobble shown is the one described in the pattern but it could easily be substituted with a different one or an applied embellishment such as a button, bead, or small fabric flower.

Cast on 15 stitches.
- **Row 1** P10, K5.
- **Row 2** (RS) P3, yo, P2tog, K6, make bobble, K3.
- **Row 3** P10, K5.
- **Row 4** P3, yo, P2tog, K10.
- **Row 5** P10, K2, P3.
- **Row 6** K3, yo, P2tog, K1, C8F, K1.
- **Row 7** P10, K2, P3.
- **Row 8** K3, yo, P2tog, K10.

SHORT-ROW FRILL

The short-row section could be inserted into many stitch patterns for an edging which will echo an element from the main fabric.

Repeat the last eight rows until the desired length is reached. Bind off.

Triangle edge

Inspired by the entrelac pattern on page 114, this simple edging looks lovely unadorned or embellished with buttons or embroidery. Working more repeats before binding off the stitches will produce a wider and deeper edging. To ensure that the last triangle finishes as required, divide the edge to be worked into sections and calculate, using a gauge swatch of the yarn to be worked, how many row repeats are needed in each section before binding off.

Working the triangle edge

With the right side of the project facing, working right to left, pick up and knit two stitches, turn and purl two stitches. Turn, knit stitches on the needle and pick up and knit one stitch along the edge, turn and purl all the stitches on the needle. Continue to turn, knit, pick up and knit, turn, purl until 10 stitches have been purled. Bind off the stitches until only one stitch loop remains and it is on the right-hand needle. Then pick up and knit two stitches along the edge and repeat the sequence until the edge has triangles along its length.

I-CORD EDGE

This i-cord technique encases and stiffens the edge and is useful for disguising any baggy edge stitches or creating a more sculptural scarf.

TRIANGLE EDGE

This edging is based on the first base row of entrelac but the first tier of squares could not also be worked.

I-cord edge

This can be worked over 4–7 stitches and encases the edge around which it is worked. It is not turned and the stitches are always worked from right to left, with the right side facing.

Working the i-cord edge

Using double-pointed needles, cast on 5 stitches and knit the first row. Then, pick up and knit a stitch through the bottom edge of the project and slide the stitches to the right of the double-pointed needle. Work the stitch nearest the point of the needle and pull the yarn firmly to draw this stitch toward the previous stitch worked, on the left of the group of stitches. Knit until two stitches remain on the left-hand needle, knit two stitches together, then pick up and knit a stitch through the edge of the project. Continue until the entire project edge is encased. Bind off the stitches.

Fringes

A fringe or tassel gives a scarf movement and the drama of a swish. They needn't be very long but they do punctuate the end of a scarf beautifully.

Fringes, tassels, and pom-poms are often an afterthought. After a scarf has been knitted, it is easier to see how a finished scarf hangs and what finishing details are required. Fringes, tassels, and pom-poms are very yarn-hungry though, so it is important to make a fringe or tassel for your project gauge swatch as soon as possible. Use this to calculate how much yarn will be required and buy extra yarn if necessary. It doesn't matter if it is a different dye lot because the texture will disguise any slight color variation.

If the yarn is no longer available then experiment with a contrasting yarn—fringes and tassels often make a successful design feature so the difference can look intentional.

Fringes can be made from most yarns. Fluffy yarns will produce a fluffy light fringe and bulky yarns will produce a more solid fringe. A dense, solid fringe can be made or a few strands can be grouped along an edge. The strands can be knotted or weighted with beads. A dense fringe can cause the edge to splay and ripple slightly. Experiment on the project gauge swatch until the desired effect is achieved.

Illusion of thickness

As with streaked hair, a mixture of tonally different yarns will make the fringe look thicker.

Making a fringe

Cut a piece of card twice the depth of the desired fringe. Wrap the yarn around the card 20–30 times, but not so many times that a thick yarn layer develops. Then, cut the yarn along both edges to produce yarn lengths double the depth of the fringe. Insert a crochet hook, either from front to back or back to

RIBBON AND ROSES FRINGE
Roses and leaf motifs hang beyond the edge to add more interest.

STRIPED FRINGE
A fringe matching the row colors was applied along the selvage of the Classic Stripes scarf page 90.

CAST-ON BIND-OFF FRINGE
This fringe has been worked with fronds of the same length, but for an alternative look vary the length of the fronds and bead the ends.

front, through a stitch or through the space between two stitches along the edge to be fringed. Fold a few strands of yarn in half and loop the fold over the crochet hook. Draw the crochet hook and the loop of yarn through the edge, wrap the yarn ends over the hook and draw them through the loop to secure the fringe in place. Repeat along the edge as required. Then place the scarf on a flat surface and, with a sharp pair of scissors, trim the fringe ends. For an even fringe work either front to back or back to front in each case and with equal spacing between the strands of the fringe.

Ribbon and roses fringe

This idea is based on the Cables and Baubles scarf on page 64. To create the effect, the scarf is worked in a finer yarn with more stitch pattern repeats. Ribbon is then threaded through the eyelets and allowed to hang free from the edge. Roses and leaf motifs (see pages 132–133) are also added for extra interest.

Cast-on/bind-off fringe

This fringe is worked as an edging. Using a gauge swatch, calculate how many stitches are required to create a fringe of the desired depth. Cast on this number of stitches, bind off all but 3–4 stitches and work a few rows on these stitches.

For this sample, cast on 30 stitches, bind off 26 stitches and knit to the end of the row. Then, knit 3 rows, and repeat until the desired length is reached.

Cast-on/bind-off twisted fringe

This fringe is worked like the cast-on/bind-off edging above but as the stitches are bound off, knit two stitches together.

Tassels

Like fringes, tassels can be made from most yarns—although the fluffier the yarn the more luscious the tassel will be. Tassels are slightly heavier than fringes so are best used sparingly.

POM-POM TASSEL

Make a tassel skirt, wind and cut a pom-pom and use the tassel skirt to secure the pom-pom. These pom-poms have been attached to the edge of the Dropped and Wrapped scarf on page 46.

Cut a piece of card to the same depth as the desired tassel. Wrap the yarn around the card until the yarns is the desired thickness for the tassel skirt. Cut a length of yarn and thread through a needle. Pass half this length of yarn under the wrapped yarn and tie it around the tassel at the top edge of the card. Cut along the bottom edge and remove the card from the skirt. To create the tassel head, pass the threaded needle 1½ in (3.5 cm) down through the tassel, wrap the yarn around the tassel once, and pass the needle behind and over the point of the start of the wrap. Wrapping in the opposite direction, wrap the tassel as many times as desired and secure the end.

To finish, trim the ends with a sharp pair of scissors.

Pom-poms

Pom-poms can be tight and dense or light and airy; they can be small and neat or large and exuberant. They can be sewn to an edge or hang free from a cord. Pom-poms need not be shy.

Making a pom-pom

There are many brands of pom-pom makers on the market but the easiest method is to use two donut-shaped circles of card. Start by determining the size of the pom-pom, then draw two circles using a compass about 10 percent larger than the desired pom-pom. Use the compass again to draw two smaller circles in the center of the first two circles. The larger these holes are, the denser the pom-pom; the smaller the holes are, the looser the pom-pom and the more likely it is to be slightly oval-shaped.

Cut out the donut shapes from the card and, holding them together, wind yarn around the card until the center hole is filled. Then, using a sharp pair of scissors and cutting a few strands at a time, cut around the pom-pom edge between the two disks. Prise the disks apart and tie a length of yarn tightly around the center of the pom-pom. Remove the disks; it may be necessary to cut them. Tousle the yarn strands into place and trim the pom-pom to make a neat ball.

VARIED COLOR
Pom-poms look great made with variegated or self-striping yarn.

Flowers and leaves

This ever-popular decorative theme is popular because it is easy to make it look good. As with all embellishment, choose a fiber that will produce the desired effect, work in colors sympathetic to the scarf or shawl or in colors that work well with a favorite outfit. Attach the motif shapes carefully so that they can be changed from time to time. The only note of caution is that too many motifs may make the piece too heavy and distort the knitted fabric.

Leaves

This leaf-like shape looks wonderful applied in a thick layer along an edge or worked in bulky yarn as a skinny scarf.

Cast on 5 stitches.
- **Row 1 (RS)** K2, yo, k1, yo, K2 (7 sts).
- **Row 2 and all even-numbered rows** K1, P to the last stitch, K1.
- **Row 3** K3, yo, K1, yo, K3 (9 sts).
- **Row 5** K4, yo, K1, yo, K4. (11 sts).
- **Row 7** K5, yo, K1, yo, K5. (13 sts).
- **Row 9** K6, yo, K1, yo, K6. (15 sts).
- **Row 11** K7, yo, K1, yo, K7 (17 sts).
Starting with a purl row, work 7 rows of stockinette stitch, knitting the first and last stitch of each row.
- **Row 19** Skpo, K to the last 2 stitches, K2tog (15 sts).
- **Row 20** K1, P to the last stitch, K1.
Repeat rows 19–20 until 3 stitches remain.
- **Row 31** Slip 2 stitches together, K1, psso.
Fasten off.

RED ROSE
A single motif on a scarf or shawl that falls around the shoulders makes a lovely finishing touch. This mohair rose has been attached to Hubby's Scarf, page 54.

Roses

The rose motif is particularly interesting because it is a long coil that can also be extended and sewn to an edge. The easiest way to work this pattern is with two circular needles or a circular needle and a double-pointed needle of the same size. The circular needle acts like a flexible stitch holder.

Larger rose

Cast on 11 stitches.

- **Row 1** (RS) [K1, P1] to the last stitch, K1.
- **Row 2** [P1, k1] to the last stitch, P1.
  Slip the first 2 stitches worked of the row 2 onto a circular needle.

The stitches on the circular needle are not worked again until the bind-off row.

- **Row 3** [K1, P1, yo] to the last stitch, K1.
- **Row 4** P1, [K1tbl, K1, P1] to the end of the row.

Slip the first 3 stitches worked of row 4 onto a circular needle.

- **Row 5** [K1, P2, yo] to the last stitch, K1.
- **Row 6** P1, [K1tbl, K2, P1] to the end of the row.

Slip the first 3 stitches worked of the row 6 onto a circular needle.

- **Row 7** [P2, yo] 4 times, P2.
- **Row 8** Knit.

Slip the first 3 stitches worked of the row 8 onto a circular needle.

Repeat rows 7–8, fitting as many repeats into the odd-numbered row as the number of stitches allows and slipping 3 stitches onto the circular needle after each even-numbered row, until there are 11 blocks of stitches or 32 stitches on the circular needle and 22 rows have been worked.

Bind off all the stitches on both needles. Coil the length around a finger and secure the layers at the base.

Smaller rose

Work as for larger rose but repeat rows 7–8, fitting as many repeats into the odd-numbered row as the number of stitches allows and slipping 3 stitches onto the circular needle after each even-numbered row, until there are 9 blocks of stitches or 26 stitches on the circular needle and 18 rows have been worked.

More flowers and leaves

From the leaf pattern (left) a variety of leaves can be made just by altering the type of increases and the size of the leaf before the stitches are decreased. Or it could be the petal of a flower with a single layer of petals or a double layer.

Cast on 3 stitches.

- **Row 1 (RS)** K1, yo, K1, yo, K1 (5 sts).

WHITE ROSES
These motifs tone with the scarf fabric to make a subtle addition to the scarf design.

COLORS AND FIBERS
When selecting a motif, work the same motif in a variety of fibers and colors.

YELLOW FLOWER

The petals of this flower pattern are based on the leaf pattern on the previous page. The button in the center is secured and loops of yarn are worked through the buttonholes, secured to the base and cut.

- **Row 2 and all even-numbered rows**
  Slip 1 stitch purlwise, P to the last st, slip 1 stitch purlwise.

Work as the leaf pattern above from rows 1–12 but on each even-numbered row, slip the first st purlwise, P to the last st, slip the last stitch purlwise.

- **Row 21** Skpo, K to the last 2 stitches, K2tog (15 sts).
- **Row 22** Slip 1 stitch purlwise, P to the last st, slip 1 stitch purlwise.

Repeat rows 21–22 until 3 stitches remain.

- **Row 33** Slip 2 stitches together, K1, psso.

Fasten off.

Star flower

The petals of this flower motif are completed one after the other in one curving piece. This is an excellent flower motif when you don't know how big or how full you want the final motif. This stitch pattern also works well as an edging or as a skinny scarf.

Cast on 10 stitches.

- ****Row 1** Purl.
- **Row 2 (RS)** K1, M1, K to the last 3 stitches, K2tog, K1.

Repeat rows 1–2 three more times.

- **Row 9** Purl.
- **Row 10** Bind off until 1 stitch loop remains on the right-hand needle.

STAR FLOWER

The number of petals in this flower can be varied to alter the fullness of the motif. A large glass bead has been placed in the center but a small pom-pom or a button would work well too.

Pick up and knit 9 stitches along the left selvage of the piece just completed.
Repeat from ** 11 more times.
Fasten off.
Seam the left selvage of the piece just completed, to the right selvage of the first piece completed.

Bobbles and cords

The neutrality of bobble and cords make them subtle decorative devices. Bobbles are very useful for correcting errors in the knitted fabric or adding a bit more texture to a finished project, while cords can be wound into more complex shapes than a knitter may be able to neatly manage. To maintain their subtlety, work in matching yarn but to create an impact choose from the wealth of texture, color, and fibers available.

I-cord

An I-cord looks like French knitting but is worked with double-pointed needles over 4–7 stitches. The work is not turned and the stitches are always worked from right to left with the right side facing.

Using double-pointed needles cast on five stitches and knit the first row. Then, slide the stitches to the right of the double-pointed needle, work the stitch nearest the point of the needle and pull the yarn firmly to drawn this stitch towards the previous stitch worked—on the left of the group of stitches. Knit the remaining 4 stitches. Continue until the desired length is reached. Bind off the stitches.

Knitted balls

This pattern for stuffed knitted balls is easily adapted to make balls of any size or stitch pattern. Continue in the increase pattern set in the pattern below, work about half the number of increase rows without any shaping, then decrease in the pattern set. This will vary slightly depending on the stitch pattern; however the shape can also be adjusted as the ball is stuffed. For a seamless ball, use double-pointed needles.

Cast on 5 stitches.
- **Row 1** (RS) Kfb 4 times, K1 (9 sts).
- **Row 2 and all even-numbered rows** Purl.
- **Row 3** K1, [M1, K1] 8 times (17 sts).
- **Row 5** K1, [M1, K2] 8 times (25 sts). Starting with a purl row, work 5 rows of stockinette stitch, knitting the first and last stitch of each row.
- **Row 11** K1, [K2tog, K1] 8 times (17 sts).
- **Row 13** K1, K2tog 8 times (9 sts).

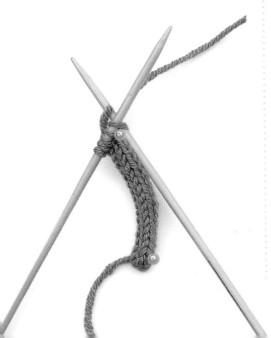

I-CORD
Work an I-cord on bamboo needles to have an extra grip on the stitch loops.

I-CORD TWIST
The beauty of an I-cord is its ability to twist and turn where a knitter might fear to tread. Here, knitted balls have been attached to end of the I-cord.

KNITTED BALLS

The ball on the right has stripes of a contrasting yarn worked on rows 6, 8, and 10. For a string of balls, the pattern was adapted for double-pointed needles, working in the round, and lengths of I-cord were worked between each ball.

■ **Row 14** K1, K2tog 4 times (5 sts). Cut the yarn and thread through a needle. Pass the yarn through the remaining stitches and fasten off. Join the two side edges, stuffing the ball lightly before closing the seam.

Bobbles

The perfect afterthought decoration, these bobbles can be made from squares of knitted fabric, gathered around their perimeter to create a nugget of knitting. Stitch patterns and gauge can be varied to produce bobbles of different weights and textures.

For the sample shown, cast on 11 stitches. Working in rows, work a square of seed stitch fabric; bind off.

Work a line of running stitch around its outer edge and draw the edges together. Attach-later bobbles can be stuffed but usually they look better without stuffing.

ATTACH-LATER BOBBLES

In the attach-later bobble cable sample left, the bobbles are sewn to this variation of the Lattice Cable scarf on page 66. Both are worked in worsted-weight yarn.

ATTACH-LATER FLOWER DESIGN

Attach-later bobbles and cords made by casting on a run of stitches and then binding them off have been used to create this floral design at the end of Hubby's Scarf on page 54.

Buttons

Buttons can be used as fasteners, as *faux* fasteners and, like beads, as decoration—in fact beads can be used as buttons. With a mind open to button suggestions, the worlds of vintage clothing, craft, and haberdashery provide a wealth of opportunities and ideas.

BEADED BUTTON
The beads in this button could have been knitted in place but the stretching of the fabric around the button can make this unpredictable, so these beads were sewn onto the knitted fabric.

COVERED BUTTON
A button can be covered with a square of knitted fabric. The fabric weight should be proportionate to the size of the button but for a small button it is no hardship even to knit with embroidery cotton. Knit a square to approximately the right size, work a line of running stitch around its outer edge and use the stretch of the fabric to gather it around a button or button-blank.

CONTRASTING THREAD
Secure the button to the fabric with a contrasting yarn.

BEADED THREAD
Use the securing thread to embellish a plain button with beads.

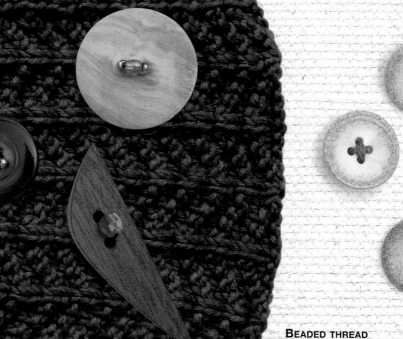

STACKED BUTTONS

The choice in large buttons can be quite limited. One solution is to choose a plain and lightweight larger button and secure a more decorative flat button on top.

BUTTON OR BEAD

This flat bead makes an excellent button. A smaller bead has been used to keep the larger bead in place.

BEER CAP

Be inventive with your choice of buttons. This button is a filed-smooth bottle cap.

Resources

Yarn companies and suppliers

Artyarns
White Plains, NY
www.artyarns.com

Blue Sky Alpacas
Cedar MN 55011
www.blueskyalpacas.com

Karabella Yarns
New York, New York
www.karabellayarns.com

Lorna's Laces
http://www.lornaslaces.net/

Paper Source
Chicago, IL
www.paper-source.com

Spud and Chloe
Cedar, Minnesota
www.spudandchloe.com

Tahki Stacy Charles
New York, New York
www.tahkistacycharles.com

Index

Credits

Hair and make-up Julia Wade
Models Camilla Hedgeland, Catherine Morse, Duncan Mias at
Needhams Models

Acknowledgements

Thank you to my eager and always ready sample knitters Maureen
Sanders and Donna Jarvis.

Thanks to Blue Sky Alpaca, Spud and Chloe, Lorna Laces,
Karabella Yarns, Artyarns, and Tahki Stacy Charles for donated yarn
for all these beautiful scarves.

Also a special thanks to my family, Alan, Nora, Cole, and
Oonagh, for allowing me to work on lace and cable patterns when
they wanted me at the park. I promise to make it up with warm
scarves this winter while we all play at the park!

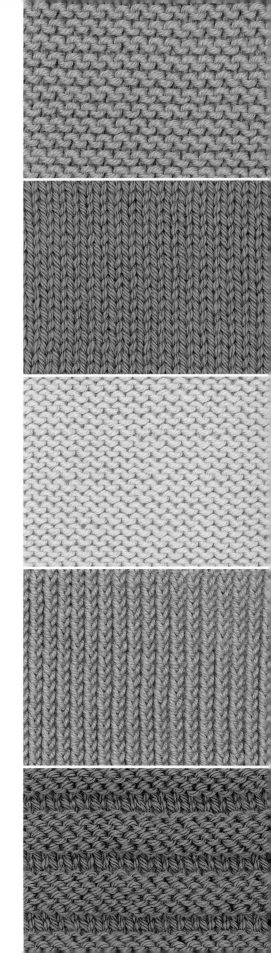